Nuffield Primary Scienc[e]
SCIENCE PROCESSES AND CONCEPT EXPLORATI[ON]

Living things in their environment

Ages
7-12

TEACHERS' GUIDE

PUBLISHED FOR THE NUFFIELD–CHELSEA CURRICULUM TRUST BY COLLINS EDUCATIONAL

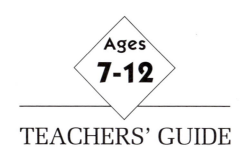

NUFFIELD PRIMARY SCIENCE
Science Processes and Concept Exploration

Directors
Paul Black
Wynne Harlen

Deputy Director
Terry Russell

Project members
Robert Austin
Derek Bell
Adrian Hughes
Ken Longden
John Meadows
Linda McGuigan
Jonathan Osborne
Pamela Wadsworth
Dorothy Watt

First published 1993 by Collins Educational
An imprint of HarperCollins*Publishers*
77-85 Fulham Palace Road
London W6 8JB

Second edition published 1995

ISBN 0 00 310258 0

Printed and bound by Scotprint Ltd, Musselburgh

Design by Carla Turchini, Chi Leung
Illustrations by Hemesh Alles, John Booth, Gay Galsworthy, Maureen Hallahan, Mary Lonsdale, Sally Neave, Theresa O'Brian
Cover artwork by Karen Tushingham

Photograph acknowledgements
Page 28: Natural History Photographic Agency
Page 60: Frank Lane Picture Agency
Page 72-3: Harry Smith Horticultural Photographic Collection, John Birdsall
Page 89: John Birdsall
Page 92: Frank Lane Picture Agency

Commissioned photography by Oliver Hatch

The Trust and the Publishers would like to thank the governors, staff and pupils of Hillbrook Primary School, Tooting, for their kind co-operation with many of the photographs in this book.

Safety adviser
Peter Borrows

Other contributors
Elizabeth Harris
Carol Joyes
Anne de Normanville
Ralph Hancock

Contents

Explanation of symbols in the margins

!	Warning
AT 1	Good opportunities to develop and assess work related to Experimental and Investigative Science
t	Notes which may be useful to the teacher
v	Vocabulary work
it	Opportunities for children to use information technology
e	Equipment needed
pb	Reference to the pupils' books

CHAPTER 1

Introduction

1.1 The SPACE approach to teaching and learning science

A primary class where the SPACE approach to science is being used may not at first seem different from any other class engaged in science activities; in either, children will be mentally and physically involved in exploring objects and events in the world around them. However, a closer look will reveal that both the children's activities and the teacher's role differ from those found in other approaches. The children are not following instructions given by others; they are not solving a problem set them by someone else. They are deeply involved in work which is based on their own ideas, and they have taken part in deciding how to do it.

The teacher has, of course, prepared carefully to reach the point where children try out their ideas. She or he will have started on the topic by giving children opportunities to explore from their own experience situations which embody important scientific ideas. The teacher will have ensured that the children have expressed their ideas about what they are exploring, using one or more of a range of approaches – from whole class discussion to talking with individual children, or asking children to write or draw – and will have explored the children's reasons for having those ideas.

With this information the teacher will have decided how to help the children to develop or revise their ideas. That may involve getting the children to use the ideas to make a prediction, then testing it by seeing if it works in practice; or the children may gather further evidence to discuss and think about. In particular, the teacher will note how 'scientific' children have been in their gathering and use of evidence; and should, by careful questioning, encourage greater rigour in the use of scientific process skills.

It is essential that the children change their ideas only as a result of what they find themselves, not by merely accepting ideas which they are told are better.

By carefully exploring children's ideas, taking them seriously and choosing appropriate ways of helping the children to test them, the teacher can move children towards ideas which apply more widely and fit the evidence better – those which are, in short, more scientific.

You will find more information about the SPACE approach in the Nuffield Primary Science *Science Co-ordinators' handbook*.

1.2 Useful strategies

Finding out children's ideas

This guide points out many opportunities for finding out children's ideas. One way is simply by talking, but there are many others. We have found the following strategies effective. How you use them may depend on the area of science you are dealing with. In Chapter 3 you will find examples of these strategies. More information about them is given in the *Science Co-ordinators' handbook.*

Talking and open questioning

Whole class discussions can be useful for sharing ideas, but they do not always give all children a chance to speak. It is often helpful if children are allowed to think of their own ideas first, perhaps working them out in drawings, and are then encouraged to share these with others – perhaps with just one other child, or with a larger group.

Annotated drawings

Asking children to draw their ideas can give a particularly clear insight into what they think. It also gives you a chance to discuss the children's ideas with them. Words conveying these ideas can then be added to the drawing, either by you or by the child. Such work can be kept as a permanent record.

Sorting and classifying

This can be a useful way of helping children to clarify their ideas and to record their thinking. They could sort a collection of objects or pictures into groups.

Writing down ideas

Children may instead write down their responses to questions you pose. Writing gives children the opportunity to express their own views, which can then be shared with others or investigated further.

Log books and diaries

These can be used to record changes over a longer investigation. They need not necessarily be kept by individual children, but could be kept by a whole group or class. Children can jot down their ideas, as words or drawings, when they notice changes, recording their reasons for what they observe.

Helping children to develop their ideas

Letting children test their own ideas

This will involve children in using some or all of the process skills of science:

- observing
- measuring
- hypothesizing
- predicting
- planning and carrying out fair tests
- interpreting results and findings
- communicating

It is an important strategy which can, and should, be used often. The *use* of process skills *develops* them – for example, through greater attention to detail in observing, more careful control of variables in fair tests, and taking all the evidence into account in interpreting the results.

Encouraging generalization from one context to another

Does an explanation proposed for a particular event fit one which is not exactly the same, but which involves the same scientific concept? You or the children might suggest other contexts that might be tried. This might be done by discussing the evidence for and against the explanation, or by gathering more evidence and testing the idea in the other context, depending on children's familiarity with the events being examined.

Discussing the words children use to describe their ideas

Children can be asked to be quite specific about the meaning of words they use, whether scientific or not. They can be prompted to think of alternative words which have almost the same meaning. They can discuss, where appropriate, words which have special meaning in a scientific context, and so be helped to realize the difference between the 'everyday' use of some words and the scientific one.

Extending the range of evidence

Some of the children's ideas may be consistent with the evidence at present available to them, but could be challenged by extending the range of evidence. This applies particularly to things which are not easily observed, such as slow changes; or those which are normally hidden, such as the insides of objects. Attempts to make these imperceptible things perceptible, often by using secondary sources, help children to consider a wider range of evidence.

Getting children to communicate their ideas

Expressing ideas in any way – through writing, drawing, modelling or, particularly, through discussion – involves thinking them through, and often rethinking and revising them. Discussion has a further advantage in that it is two-way and children can set others' ideas against their own. Just realizing that there are different ideas helps them to reconsider their own.

1.3 Equal opportunities

The SPACE approach to teaching and learning science gives opportunities for every child to build on and develop his or her experiences, skills and ideas. It can therefore be used to benefit pupils of all kinds and at any stage of development. This is fully discussed in the *Science Co-ordinators' handbook*.

1.4 Living things in their environment and the curriculum

This teachers' guide is divided into four themes; in each one there is a section on finding out children's ideas, examples of ideas children have, and a section on helping children to develop their ideas.

Nuffield Primary Science Themes

Habitats and environmental change

This theme explores the variety of places in which animals and plants live and the ways in which organisms are affected by changes in their environment. In general terms, children are aware that organisms of different types tend to live in different kinds of places and that the prevailing conditions affect the animals and plants. However, these ideas tend not to be well developed and specific links are rarely made. The activities encourage children to investigate particular environments in some detail and to observe, measure and record the changes that take place over a period of time in both the non-living and the living parts of the environment. Discussions of the findings consider how and why the changes take place. These activities form a basis for developing an understanding of interactions between living things and their environment.

Feeding relationships between organisms

This theme introduces some of the ways in which living things interact with each other. In particular it explores the relationship between organisms through their feeding patterns. Children generally recognize that all living things need food to survive and some children recognize that food originates from plants. However, this link is usually made in relation to the processing of their own food and the idea that plants get their food from the soil. The activities help children to investigate the food sources of different organisms and to develop the idea of a food chain in which plants produce food using energy from the Sun, with all other food originating from this. These activities provide a basis for developing the idea of a food web and that of an ecosystem.

Waste and decay

The aim of this theme is to develop ideas about what happens to dead plant and animal matter as well as what happens to the waste materials produced by human activity. Children recognize that something happens to dead organisms (they might just disappear or rot), but rarely mention how or why this happens. Very few children appear to be aware of the role played by micro-organisms in the process of decay. Ideas about waste materials vary enormously and include suggestions that rubbish goes to the tip to be burnt or recycled. The suggested activities investigate what happens to a range of materials in different conditions and examine the ways in which waste is treated. Tests to investigate the specific conditions needed for decay to occur help to develop the ideas and provide a basis for further understanding.

Effects of human activity on the environment

This theme aims to help children understand the variety of ways in which human activity affects the environment and to recognize some of the effects caused by particular activities. Children recognize ways in which parts of the environment have been changed by people but tend to have restricted views about the extent of human influence. Some young children express ideas that people have made everything. The activities encourage children to link human activities and their effects more closely through observations, surveys and by getting directly involved with local projects. Wider issues relating to pollution, and global effects (e.g. the greenhouse effect) are also considered using secondary source materials and discussions.

National Curriculum Programmes of Study	Environmental Studies 5-14 (Scotland): Science
Life Processes and Living Things **1 Life processes** **a** that there are life processes, including nutrition, movement, growth and reproduction, common to animals, including humans; **b** that there are life processes, including growth, nutrition, and reproduction, common to plants. **5 Living things in their environment** **a** that different plants and animals are found in different habitats; **b** how animals and plants in two different habitats are suited to their environment.	**Understanding Living Things and the Processes of Life (Stages P4 to P6)** **The processes of life** • the structure and functions of the parts of flowering plants and factors which affect germination and growth; **Interaction of living things with their environment** • how plants and animals are affected by environmental conditions.
Life Processes and Living Things **1 Life processes** **a** that there are life processes, including nutrition, movement, growth and reproduction, common to animals, including humans; **b** that there are life processes, including growth, nutrition, and reproduction, common to plants. **5 Living things in their environment** **b** how animals and plants in two different habitats are suited to their environment; **c** that food chains show feeding relationships in an ecosystem; **d** that nearly all food chains start with a green plant.	**Understanding Living Things and the Processes of Life (Stages P4 to P6)** **Interaction of living things with their environment** • simple food chains based on energy from the Sun.
Life Processes and Living Things **5 Living things in their environment** **e** that micro-organisms exist, and that many may be beneficial, while others may be harmful.	**Understanding Living Things and the Processes of Life (Stages P4 to P6)** **Interaction of living things with their environment** • the importance of conservation and the value of re-cycling materials.
This theme now appears in the Geography National Curriculum at Key Stage 2. Pupils should be taught how people affect the environment.	**Understanding Living Things and the Processes of Life (Stages P4 to P6)** **Interaction of living things with their environment** • the importance of conservation and the value of re-cycling materials; • the interaction between humans and their environment.

1.5 Experimental and Investigative Science

Two important aspects of children's learning in science are:

- learning how to investigate the world around them;
- learning to make sense of the world around them using scientific ideas.

These are reflected in the National Curriculum. 'Experimental and Investigative Science' covers the first aspect. The second aspect is covered by the rest of the Programme of Study. Although these two aspects of science learning are separated in the National Curriculum they cannot be separated in practice and it is not useful to try to do so. Through investigation children explore their ideas and/or test out the ideas which arise from discussion. As a result, ideas may be advanced, but this will depend on the children's investigation skills. Thus it is important to develop these skills in the context of activities which extend ideas. So there is no separate Nuffield Primary Science teachers' guide on scientific investigations, because opportunities to make these occur throughout all the guides and they form an essential part of the SPACE approach.

Thus in this guide you will find investigations which provide opportunities to develop and assess the skills and understanding set out in Experimental and Investigative Science. These are marked in the text by the symbol shown here. In this teachers' guide, the investigations which cover the most skills are 'What do plants and animals need to live?' (page 47), 'Conditions affecting the decay of materials' (page 83) 'Things that are thrown away' (page 87), and 'How can we reduce the amount of waste?' (page 90).

AT 1

It is important that teachers give active guidance to pupils during investigations to help them work out how to improve the way in which they plan and carry out their investigations.

Experimental and Investigative Science is about the ways scientific evidence can be obtained, about the ways observations and measurements are made, and about the way in which the evidence is analysed. It therefore sets out three main ways in which pupils can develop their ability to do experimental and investigative science, as follows:-

1 'Planning experimental work'. Here, children should be helped to make progress from asking general and vague questions, to suggesting ideas which could be tested. Teachers' discussion with pupils should aim to help them to make predictions, using their existing understanding, on the basis of which they can decide what evidence should be collected. This should lead them to think about what apparatus and equipment they should use.

When children describe plans for their work, they should be helped to think about what features they are going to change, what effects of these changes they are going to observe or measure, and what features they must keep the same. In this way they can come to understand what is meant by 'a fair test'.

2 'Obtaining evidence'. Children should make observations in the light of their ideas about what they are looking for and why. When they describe their observations, teachers may have to help them to improve, for example by reminding them of their original aims and plan for the work. Such help should also encourage progress from qualitative comparisons and judgements to appreciating the value of making quantitative measurements (for example 'cold water' is qualitative, 'water at 12°C' is quantitative). This should lead to the development of skills with a variety of instruments and to increasing care and accuracy in measurement, involving, for example, repeating measurements to check.

3 'Considering evidence'. Here, children should first learn to record their evidence in systematic and clear ways, starting with simple drawings and then learning to use tables, bar charts and line graphs to display the patterns in numerical data. Then they should be asked to think about and discuss their results, considering what might be learnt from any trends or patterns. As ideas develop, they should be careful in checking their evidence against the original idea underlying the investigation and should become increasingly critical in discussing alternative explanations which might fit their evidence. In such discussions, they should be helped to relate their arguments to their developing scientific understanding. They should also be guided to see possibilities for conducting their investigation more carefully, or in quite different ways.

Whilst these three may seem to form a natural sequence of stages, children's work might not follow this particular sequence. For example, some might start with evidence from their observations and proceed on this basis to propose a hypothesis and a plan to test it. For others, the results of one task may be the starting point for a new inquiry involving new measurements. Useful learning about how to investigate might arise when only one or two of the above aspects of an investigation are involved, or when the teacher tells children about some aspects so that they can concentrate on others. However, there should be some occasions for all pupils when they carry out the whole process of investigation by themselves.

The assessment examples given in chapter 4 are analysed in relation to the level descriptions, which describe children's progress in relation to these three aspects: *planning experimental work, obtaining evidence* and *considering evidence*. Thus, these three provide a framework both for guiding children and for assessing their progress in experimental and investigative work.

CHAPTER 2

Planning

2.1 Introduction: planning with children's ideas in mind

The key scientific ideas presented in this guide can be explored in various contexts, and many of the suggested activities can be incorporated into cross-curricular topic work. This chapter uses a worked example as an aid to planning a topic. Further information on planning is given in the *Science Co-ordinators' handbook.*

A teacher using the SPACE approach should take into account:

- the need to find out children's own ideas, not only at the beginning of the work but also at intervals during it;
- the importance of planning the investigations with the children, using their ideas as the starting point;
- the concepts that are being explored;
- the direction in which the children's ideas are developing.

2.2 Cross-curricular topics

Activities which explore the ideas covered in this teachers' guide to *Living things in their environment* may be approached via a number of topics in addition to the one set out as an example in the planning sheets (pages 15-16). It is assumed that teachers will adapt the topic to whatever local resources are of interest and readily to hand. Some possibilities are given below.

Around our school

There are links with work in Geography through mapping both inside and outside the buildings.
What parts of the school are considered 'natural' and which man-made?
How much rubbish is produced in the school? What is recycled?
Where did the materials for building the school come from? What effects might the production of these materials have on the environment?
Animal and plant life around the school grounds.
Create a nature garden.
History of the school site – what was there before the school?

Some links with other Nuffield Primary Science teachers' guides and pupils' books include:

The variety of life – different organisms found;
Rocks, soil and weather – landscape features, soil and rocks in school grounds;

Materials – compare and contrast the variety of materials and structure of the buildings;
Using energy – an energy audit of the school, ways of 'saving energy';
Sound and music – sounds in the environment, a listening walk;
Electricity and magnetism – the uses of electricity around the school, safety.

Conservation

Consider endangered species locally, nationally and globally.
Plan and carry out conservation tasks.
Look at historical buildings and objects.
Debate local conservation issues, such as a town planning enquiry (role-playing).
Find out about the work of museums, art galleries, heritage centres, and so on. Why do people go to them? What should places like this be doing?

Some links with other Nuffield Primary Science teachers' guides and pupils' books include:

The variety of life – different organisms in danger, and past life forms;
Rocks, soil and weather – landscape features, soils and rocks, effects of human activity on landscape, soil erosion;
Materials – compare and contrast the variety of materials and structure of the buildings;
Using energy – ways of 'saving energy', energy conservation.

In the wood

Woodlands offer children the opportunity to explore plants and animals in a natural environment.
Differences between evergreen and deciduous plants.
Use identification keys, and observe similarities and differences between plants.
The various ways in which trees flower, fruit and produce and disperse seeds could be investigated. ('Conkers' and 'helicopters' are likely to be familiar starting points.)
Light and shade in the wood, and the effect of light on the undergrowth at various stages in the life of a wood.
Animal life in leaf litter and humus.
Animals associated with trees: the presence of some animals may be inferred from the presence of nests or holes – badgers, foxes, rabbits, squirrels; and woodpeckers, wood-pigeons, and rooks all leave signs of their presence.
Evidence of seasonal change to be found in a wood, such as small flowering plants.

Some links with other Nuffield Primary Science teachers' guides and pupils' books include:

The variety of life – range of animal and plant life;
Rocks, soil and weather – landscape features, soils and rocks;
Materials – compare and contrast the variety of materials;
Light – light and shade, shadows;
The Earth in Space – causes of seasonal and daily changes.

Our town

History of industry in the area; changes in the processes used; possible sources of raw materials.
Possible sources and types of pollution.
Where do the products go to? Market research.
Public opinion survey – is there too much industry in the area? or not enough?
Designing an advertising campaign for a local firm; development of the town; tourist attractions.
The Council and the running of the town.
Buildings.

Some links with other Nuffield Primary Science teachers' guides and pupils' books include:

The variety of life – different organisms found in the parks etc.;
Rocks, soil and weather – landscape features, soils and rocks in the area;
Materials – compare and contrast the variety of materials and structure of the buildings;
Using energy – ways of 'saving energy', getting fuels to and around the town;
Sound and music – sounds in the environment, a listening walk; signs and signals;
Light – lighting the town, signs and signals;
Electricity and magnetism – the uses of electricity around the town, getting electricity to the town.

2.3 Topic plan examples

The plans on pages 15-16, illustrate how the science related to *Living things in their environment* may be embedded in a cross-curricular topic. The topic presented is 'Our town' and opportunities for exploring mathematics, language, history, geography, design technology and art have been indicated on the first plan. On the second plan the science work has been amplified to illustrate possible areas of exploration based within the overall topic. It is important to remember these are only examples and are not intended to be exhaustive.

2.4 Use of information technology

it

Specific examples of opportunities to use information technology are indicated by this symbol in the margin and referred to in the text. The examples include:

- word processing to produce reports of investigations;
- simple databases to record and analyse data collected, about rubbish, etc.;
- using sensors coupled with a computer to detect and measure temperature, for instance in a compost heap.

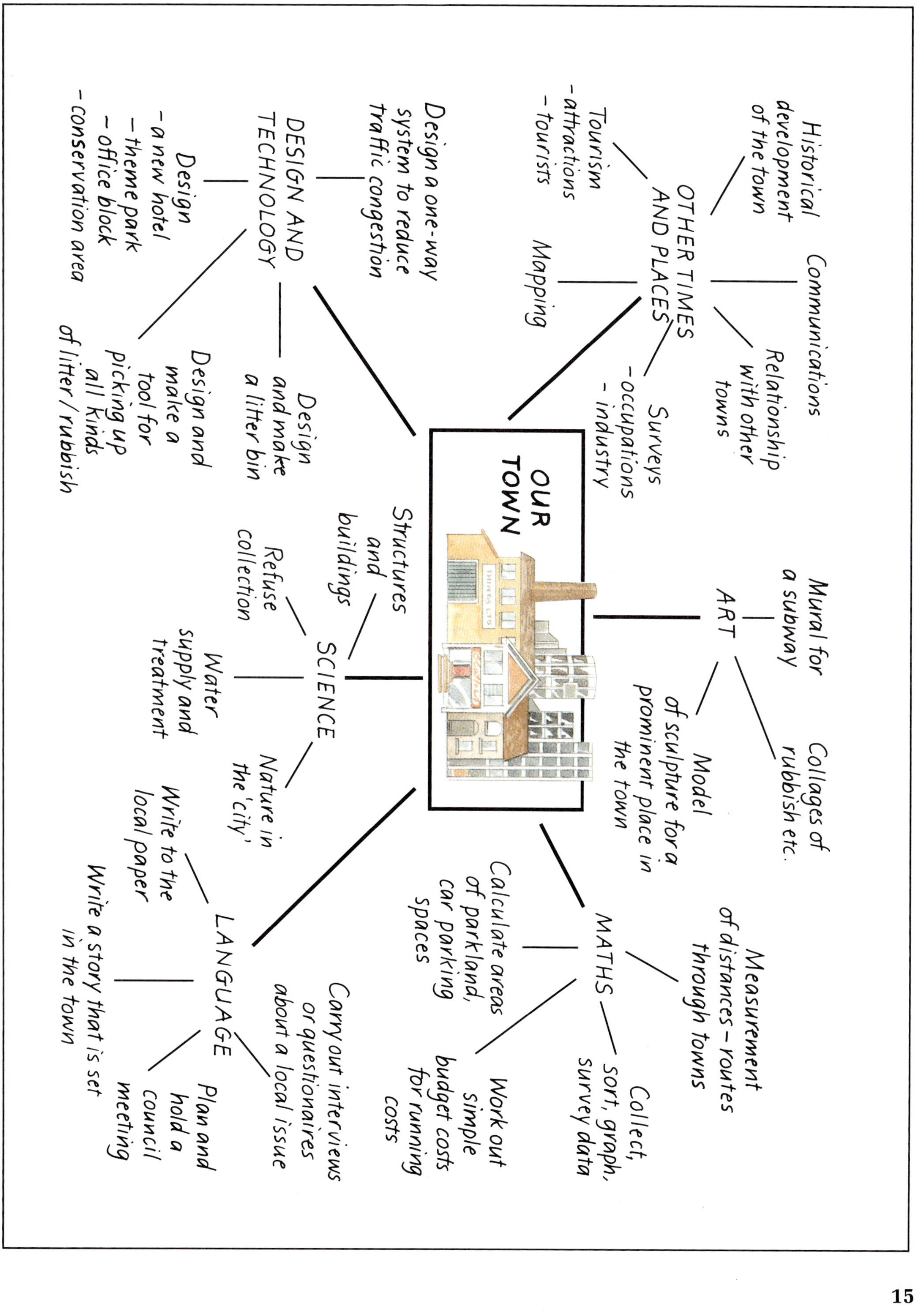
OUR TOWN
OTHER TIMES AND PLACES
Historical development of the town
Communications
Relationship with other towns
Surveys
- occupations
- industry
Mapping
Tourism
- attractions
- tourists
DESIGN AND TECHNOLOGY
Design a one-way system to reduce traffic congestion
Design
- a new hotel
- theme park
- office block
- conservation area
Design and make a litter bin
Design and make a tool for picking up all kinds of litter / rubbish
ART
Mural for a subway
Collages of rubbish etc.
Model of sculpture for a prominent place in the town
SCIENCE
Structures and buildings
Refuse collection
Water supply and treatment
Nature in the 'city'
MATHS
Measurement of distances – routes through towns
Calculate areas of parkland, car parking spaces
Collect, sort, graph, survey data
Work out simple budget costs for running costs
LANGUAGE
Write to the local paper
Write a story that is set in the town
Carry out interviews or questionaires about a local issue
Plan and hold a council meeting

Science within a cross-curricular topic

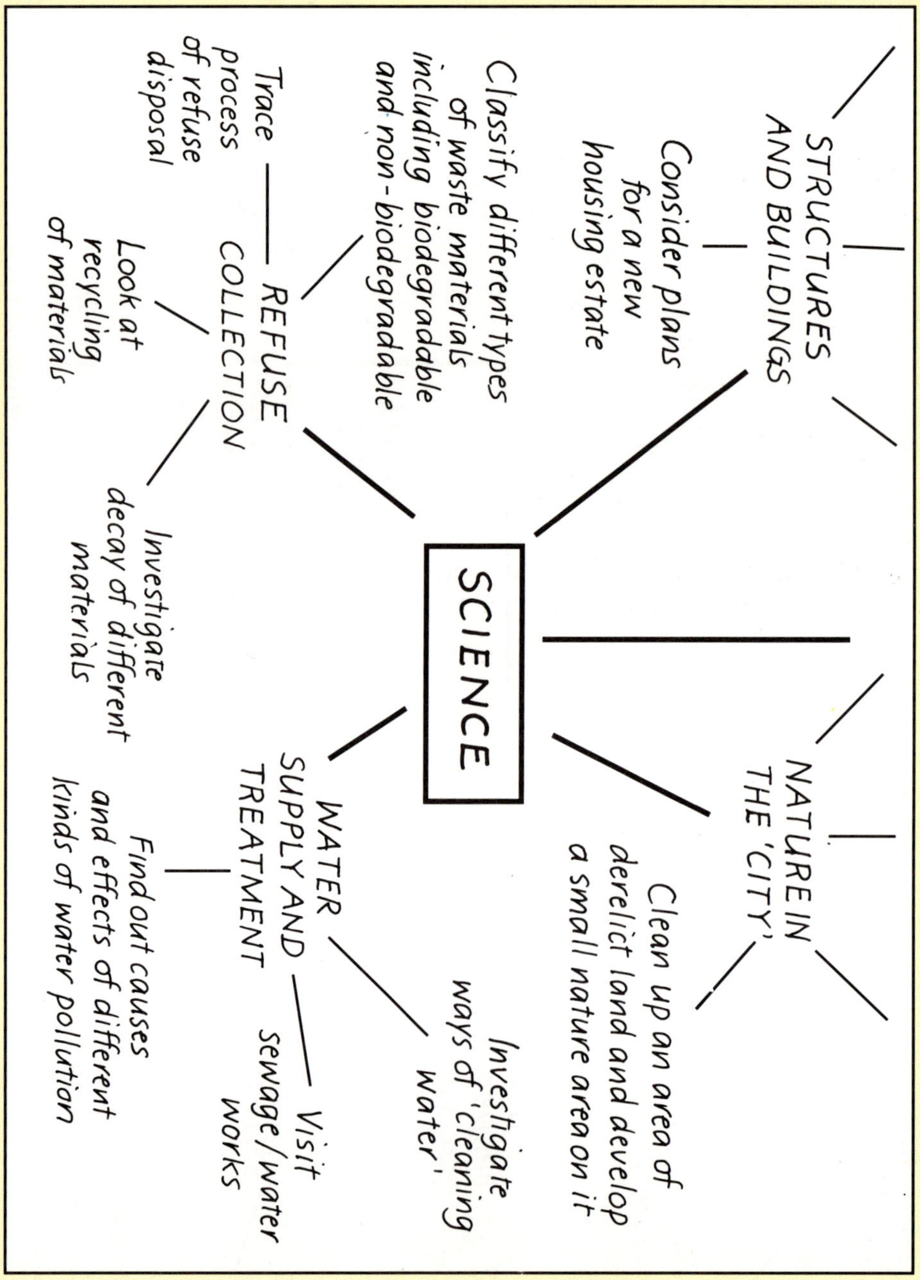
SCIENCE
STRUCTURES AND BUILDINGS
Consider plans for a new housing estate
NATURE IN THE 'CITY'
Clean up an area of derelict land and develop a small nature area on it
WATER SUPPLY AND TREATMENT
Investigate ways of 'cleaning water'
Visit sewage/water works
Find out causes and effects of different kinds of water pollution
REFUSE COLLECTION
Classify different types of waste materials including biodegradable and non-biodegradable
Trace process of refuse disposal
Look at recycling of materials
Investigate decay of different materials

2.5 Pupils' books

The pupils' books accompanying this guide are called *Habitats* for the lower juniors and *More about habitats* for the upper juniors. The pupil books are intended to be used spread by spread. The spreads are not sequential, and they are covered in these notes in thematic order.

Features of the pupil books include:

- ◆ Stimulus spreads, often visual, designed to raise questions, arouse curiosity, and to promote discussion.
- ◆ Information spreads, which give secondary source material in a clear and attractive way.
- ◆ Activity ideas, to form the basis of investigations to be carried out by the children.
- ◆ Cross-curricular spreads and stories which can act as a basis for creative writing, or spreads with a historical or creative focus.
- ◆ Real life examples of applications of science in the everyday world.

Habitats

One habitat throughout the year pages 2–3

Purpose: To provide information about seasonal changes in the same habitat throughout the year.
Pupils' book cross-references: Time and Space, pages 6-7.
Teachers' guide cross-references: Living things in their environment, pages 30–1.

In a garden pages 4–5

Purpose: To provide information about a garden as a habitat.
Extension activities: Children can use this spread and the following three related ones for identification and to work out a simple food chain. They could use the information in the boxes to sort the creatures shown into animal and vegetable eaters.
Pupils' books cross-references: Different plants and animals, pages 6-7.
Teachers' guide cross-references: Living things in their environment, pages 46, 51, 70, 83, 118-9.

In a pond pages 6–7

Purpose: To provide information about a pond as habitat.
Note: Remind children of the safety aspects of working near water.
Extension activities: Children could provide a similar picture to this, after a pond-dipping exercise, to show what they found.
Pupils' book cross-references: More about living things in action, pages 16-17.
Teachers' guide cross-references: Living things in their environment, pages 46, 51, 70, 118-9.

In the soil and under leaves pages 8–9

Purpose: To help children develop their ideas about some common mini-beasts and to provide information to identify them.

Extension activity: Compare what is on this page with the children's own findings after a minibeast hunt.
Teachers' guide cross-references: Living things in their environment, pages 46, 48, 51, 70, 118-9.

On a rocky shore pages 10–11

Purpose: To provide information about the seashore as a habitat.
Note: Not all children will have had a chance to visit the seaside.
Question for discussion: How have these creatures and plants adapted to life on the sea shore? (All the answers are on the spread.)
Teachers' guide cross-references: Living things in their environment, pages 46, 51, 70, 118-9.

A place to live pages 14–15

Purpose: To provide an opportunity for children to devise their own habitat using the pictorial information.
Extension activity: Children could explore a local habitat.
Teachers' guide cross-references: Living things in their environment, pages 47, 56–59 (for photocopiable cards), 118-9.

At home in an oak tree pages 16–17

Purpose: To provide an example of a 'micro' habitat.
Extension activities: Children could observe a tree of their own, looking out for signs of bird and animal activity. Use sweep nets or pieces of material to make a collection of the small creatures which live among the branches. The children could make their own life story books for a tree or they could make time-lines to show what was happening when the tree started to grow. The oak tree is a good example because these can be several hundred years old.
Teachers' guide cross-reference: Living things in their environment, page 55.

What's for dinner? pages 12–13

Purpose: To give an example of a simple food chain.
Notes: Examples of food chains that might be found in a field are:
grass → cow → person;
buttercup → bee;
earth worm → bird → sparrowhawk.
A food chain should start with the Sun and show the flow of energy – so the arrows on the picture on page 12 should be pointing the other way.
Extension activities: Children could devise their own food chains by using the preceding pages or by examining a local habitat. Ask, is the poem really an example of a food chain?
Teachers' guide cross-references: Living things in their environment, pages 70, 118-9.

Down the drain pages 18–19

Purpose: To show that one of the main contributors to the pollution of rivers, lakes and seas is what we throw down the drain each day.
Extension activities: Children could make their own list of what goes down their drain every day. What do they think happens to all of these things? Ask them to design their own posters about how to prevent the waterways being polluted.

Pupils' book cross-references: More about rocks, soil and weather, pages 2-3.
Teachers' guide cross-references: Living things in their environment, pages 25–6, 88, 106; *Rocks soil and weather,* page 13.

On the rubbish tip pages 20–21

Purpose: To discuss the ways in which we can pollute the environment by tipping rubbish.
Question for discussion: Which of the following can be recycled: kitchen rubbish, cans, newspapers, clothes, garden waste?
Extension activities: The class could visit a local supermarket, to see which items are collected for recycling. The children could build something using items which would otherwise be discarded.
Teachers' guide cross-references: Living things in their environment, pages 15-16, 86–70.

A recycling journey pages 22–23

Purpose: A discussion spread showing some of the ways household items are recycled.
Extension activities: Children could design a poster to encourage their friends to use the local recycling facilities. Use recycling as a basis for a class project: children could list the different ways of recycling. Ask them to think about what happens to things they throw away. They could use household waste to make something useful, such as a washing-up bottle into a pencil-holder or a musical shaker.
Pupils' book cross-references: More about materials; pages 18-19.
Teachers' guide cross-references: Living things in their environment, pages 15-16, 89.

More about habitats

It's a hard life pages 2–3

Purpose: To show how some creatures are able to adapt to exceptionally hard conditions.
Questions for discussion: Look at each picture closely. What difficulties do the animals face because of where they live? How are the animals and plants adapted?
Extension activity: The class could look at the local environment – the playground, the school building, the tarmac around it. Is it an easy or hard place for plants and animals to live?
Teachers' guide cross-references: Living things in their environment, pages 47, 55.

Wildlife in towns pages 4–5

Purpose: To provide information about an urban habitat.
Extension activities: Children could explore the buildings and playground to discover what kind of wildlife exists there. They could develop some of this information into a nature trail.
Teachers' guide cross-references: Living things in their environment, pages 14, 15-16, 46, 105.

Observing nature pages 6–7

Purpose: To provide information about the different ways of observing nature.
Note: Children should be discouraged from picking wild flowers.
Extension activity: Children could think of ways of recording their observations – by drawing, or taking photographs, for example.
Teachers' guide cross-references: Living things in their environment, pages 13, 52.

Alligator – keeper of the glades pages 20–21

Purpose: A discussion spread which describes an endangered and unusual habitat, the effect that humans have had on it.
Teachers' guide cross-references: Living things in their environment, pages 13, 51.

Surviving in the desert pages 22–23

Purpose: A discussion spread which gives an example of an unusual habitat and how animals and plants have adapted to suit it.
Notes: The spread also shows that desert is not just sand and that deserts have wildlife. However, there is much less than in the swamp on pages 20-1.
Teachers' guide cross-references: Living things in their environment, page 55.

Living together pages 8–9

Purpose: A 'wow' spread, to show another type of habitat, the co-dependence of some living creatures, and some extraordinary animal partnerships.
Questions for discussion: Who do you depend on? Who depends on you? (Pets, for example, may rely on children feeding them.) Which animals do people rely on? (Guide dogs, for example.)
Pupils' books cross-references: More about different plants and animals pages 4-5.
Teachers' guide cross-reference: Living things in their environment, page 71.

Going mouldy and rotting away pages 10–11

Purpose: To provide information about bacteria and fungi.
Notes: Children examining moulding or rotting material should be warned to be very careful with these – to try not to touch them, and always to wash their hands afterwards. Do not seal containers of rotting material too tightly.
Extension activities: Children could set up their own investigations about things going mouldy. Place bread, fruit in sealed containers and watch their progress. (Take care to label the containers with a health warning.) They could make their own compost heap.
Pupils' book cross-references: Materials, pages 16-17.
Teachers' guide cross-reference: Living things in their environment, pages 86–88.

Is it environmentally friendly? pages 18–19

Purpose: To help children argue effectively about environmental issues.
Note: The answer to the main question is that the paper cup is the most environmentally friendly as it is made from a renewable resource.
Extension activity: Children could collect packaging which gives an indication of whether it can be recycled or is biodegradable.
Teachers' guide cross-references: Living things in their environment, pages 86–7, *Materials,* pages 75, 78.

The story of Mr Carver pages 12–13

Purpose: To describe the work of a black scientist.
Extension activities: Children could find out more about slavery and why George Washington Carver's achievements are so significant.
Teachers' guide cross-references: Living things in their environment, page 104; *Rocks, soil and weather,* page 54.

Food farming pages 14–15

Purpose: To provide information about the effects humans can have on the natural environment.
Questions for discussion: Why do farmers use fertilizers? What are pesticides? What are natural pesticides? (All the answers are in the book.)
Extension activities: Discuss the term 'organic'. What does the word mean? The children could look for examples of organic foods in supermarkets.
Teachers' guide cross-reference: Living things in their environment, page 104.

Our polluted air pages 16–17

Purpose: To provide information and to explain some green issues and terms that children may have come across.
Extension activity: Children could explain their understanding of the terms 'greenhouse effect', 'ozone layer' and 'acid rain'.
Teachers' guide cross-references: Living things in their environment, pages 106–7, 123-126.

2.6 Planning your science programme in school

The following pages give examples of how two schools have planned their science programme for the whole of Key Stage 2. Planning of this kind helps to provide continuity and progression in children's learning in science. The development of such whole school programmes is discussed more fully in the *Science Co-ordinators' Handbook*.

Each plan covers the requirements for the National Curriculum at Key Stage 2 and shows which themes in the Nuffield Primary Science Teachers' Guides have been used for planning the topic in detail by the class teacher.

Example 1 (page 23)

Based in a semi-rural area this junior school has approximately 170 children on roll. There are no mixed age groups in the school. The plan provides for overlaps in order to provide opportunities for pupils to revisit concepts and build on their previous experience.

The overall curriculum is planned around topics which are history-led in the Autumn term, science-led in the Spring term and geography-led in the Summer term. Therefore, where ever possible cross-curricular links are developed, but if this becomes contrived, then subject specific mini-topics are planned. The programme only shows the Science elements taught each term.

Example 2 (page 24)

This urban school has recently reviewed its science programme in order to help encourage progression in the concepts covered and avoid repetition of the same activities. Teachers asked for guidance but also wanted the flexibility to develop the topics in a way which was appropriate to their own class.

It was also felt that some concepts, not necessarily demanded by the National Curriculum, should be covered e.g. Seasons. Therefore, suitable topics are included in the programme.

The summer term in Year 6 is free to accommodate SATs and to allow teachers time to further develop the interests of children.

Example 1

	AUTUMN TERM	SPRING TERM	SUMMER TERM
YEAR 3	The Earth and beyond/Magnetism	All about me	Service to our homes
Nuffield Primary Science Teachers' Guide	The Earth in Space 3.1, 3.2, 3.3 Electricity and magnetism 3.4	Living processes 3.1, 3.2, 3.3 The variety of life 3.2 Light 3.1	Electricity and magnetism 3.1, 3.2, 3.3 Materials 3.1 Using energy 3.2
Programme of Study †	Sc4:4a, b, c, d; Sc4:2a	Sc2: 1a; 2a, b, e, f; Sc4:3a, d	Sc3:1a, b, c; Sc4:1a, b, c
YEAR 4	Sound and music / Mechanisms	Habitats	Built environment
Nuffield Primary Science Teachers' Guide	Sound and music 3.1, 3.2 Using energy 3.3	The variety of life 3.1 Living processes 3.4 Living things in their environment 3.1, 3.2	Materials 3.2, 3.3 Using energy 3.1
Programme of Study †	Sc4:3e, f, g; Sc4:2d, e	Sc2:1b; 3a, b, c, d; 4a; Sc3:1d	Sc3:1e; 2a, b, c, d
YEAR 5	Electricity/Starting and stopping	Structures	Earth and atmosphere/ Light
Nuffield Primary Science Teachers' Guide	Electricity and magnetism 3.2, 3.3 Forces and movement 3.1, 3.2	Materials 3.1, 3.2, 3.3 Rocks, soil and weather 3.1 The variety of life 3.3	Rocks, soil and weather 3.2 The Earth in Space 3.1, 3.2, 3.3, 3.4 Light 3.2, 3.3
Programme of Study †	Sc4:1a, b, c, d; Sc4:2b, c	Sc3:1b, d; 2f; 3a, b, c, d, e	Sc3:2e; Sc4:4a, b, c, d; Sc4:3a, b, c
YEAR 6	The human body/Keeping healthy	Forces	Our environment
Nuffield Primary Science Teachers' Guide	Living processes 3.2, 3.3 The variety of life 3.2	Forces and movement 3.1, 3.2, 3.3, 3.4 Electricity and magnetism 3.4 Using energy 3.3	Living things in their environment 3.2, 3.3, 3.4
Programme of Study †	Sc2:2c, d, g, h	Sc4:2a, b, c, d, e, f, g, h	Sc2:5a, b, c, d, e

† For the purposes of these charts the references to sections of the Programme of Study have been abbreviated as follows:
Sc2 = Life Processes and Living Things
Sc3 = Materials and their Properties
Sc4 = Physical Processes

Example 2

	AUTUMN TERM		SPRING TERM		SUMMER TERM	
YEAR 3	Earth and time	Reflections and shadows	What's under our feet?	Moving things	Variety of life	Habitats
Nuffield Primary Science Teachers' Guide	The Earth in Space 3.1, 3.2	Light 3.2	Rocks, soil and weather 3.1 Living things in their environment 3.3	Forces and movement 3.1	The variety of life 3.1	Living things in their environment 3.1
Programme of Study †	Sc4:4a, b, c, d	Sc4:3a, b, c	Sc2:5e; Sc3:1d	Sc4:2a, b, c, d, e	Sc2:1a, b; 4a	Sc2:5a, b
YEAR 4	Frictional forces	Hot and cold	Materials and their properties	Sounds	Growing	Electricity
Nuffield Primary Science Teachers' Guide	Forces and movement 3.2	Using energy 3.1	Materials 3.1	Sound and music 3.1	Living processes 3.1, 3.4	Electricity and magnetism 3.1, 3.2, 3.3
Programme of Study †	Sc4:2b, c, f, g, h	Sc3:2b, c	Sc3:1a, b, e	Sc4:3e, f	Sc2:3a, b, c, d	Sc3:1c; Sc4:1a, b, c
YEAR 5	The Earth in the Solar System	Weather and its effects	Feeding relationships	Individual variation	Light sources	Sounds travelling
Nuffield Primary Science Teachers' Guides	The Earth in Space 3.1, 3.2, 3.3	Rocks, soil and weather 3.1, 3.2	Living things in their environment 3.2, 3.3	The variety of life 3.2	Light 3.1	Sound and music 3.2
Programme of Study †	Sc4:c, d	Sc3:1d, 2e	Sc2:5c, d, e	Sc2:4a; 5a	Sc4:3a, b, c, d	Sc4:3e, f, g
YEAR 6	Forces and movement	Living processes	Electricity	Materials		
Nuffield Primary Science Teachers' Guide	Forces and movement 3.3, 3.4	Living processes 3.2, 3.3	Electricity and magnetism 3.1, 3.2, 3.3	Materials 3.2, 3.3		
Programme of Study †	Sc4:2d, e, f, g, h	Sc2:2a, b, c, d, e, f, g, h	Sc4:1c, d	Sc3:2a, b, d, f; 3a, b, c, d, e		

2.7 Resources

Full use should be made of the school grounds, other areas of the local environment which are safely accessible, and places for appropriate visits if they can be arranged.

The precise nature of the resources needed at any time will, of course, depend upon the ideas that the children have and the methods of testing that they devise. However, the following list provides a general guide to the resources needed to carry out the investigations shown in this book.

Supply of plastic or rubber gloves, or plastic bags
Variety of sealable plastic containers (see-through if possible) for collection and observation of rubbish
Sealable polythene bags
(These items are needed for safety purposes.)

Sealable clear plastic containers
Thermometers
Hand lenses
Tweezers
Trowels
Spade
Water bottles for collecting samples of water
Filter papers
Sieves
Books, videos, pamphlets and posters referring to human activities including the sources and effects of pollution.
Photographs of a range of environments including ones with which the children are not familiar. These should include obvious and not so obvious features resulting from human activity.

2.8 Warnings

Activities which need particular care are indicated by this symbol in the margin. Everything possible should be done to ensure the safety of the children during their investigations. You should consult any guidelines produced by your own Local Education Authority and, if your school or LEA is a member, by CLEAPSS. See also the Association for Science Education publication *Be safe! some aspects of safety in school science and technology for Key Stages 1 and 2* (2nd edition, 1990). This contains more detailed advice than can be included here.

The points listed below require particular attention.

Care must be taken in handling litter and other forms of rubbish – protect hands with disposable gloves or plastic bags.

Consider immunization against tetanus for both teachers and children.

Mouldy material produces spores to which some people are allergic. All mouldy material should be kept in sealed containers which are not opened.

Children should wash their hands thoroughly after handling any rubbish or similar materials.

Fieldwork and visits must be carefully organized and supervised. Check your school's policy on visits.

CHAPTER 3

Exploring living things in their environment

Theme organizer

LIVING THINGS IN THEIR ENVIRONMENT

HABITATS AND ENVIRONMENTAL CHANGE 3.1

Living things live in a variety of places, which are called habitats.

Living things are suited to the places in which they live.

*Living things respond to changes in their environment.

FEEDING RELATIONSHIPS BETWEEN ORGANISMS 3.2

Living things need certain conditions to stay alive.

Plants are the ultimate source of food for all living things.

*Living things interact with each other in various ways, including competition for resources.

WASTE AND DECAY 3.3

The remains of living things will, under suitable conditions, decay; the substances released by this can be taken in and used as nutrients by other organisms.

Materials can be re-used, recycled or discarded.

Some materials change and decay quickly, while for others the changes occur over a long time.

*Many human activities produce waste materials which cause changes in the environment, locally and/or globally.

EFFECTS OF HUMAN ACTIVITY ON THE ENVIRONMENT 3.4

Human activity has changed all parts of the environment.

The resources of the Earth are finite.

(*Asterisks indicate ideas which will be developed more fully in later key stages.)

3.1

Habitats and environmental change

AREAS FOR INVESTIGATION

Children should carry out investigations of plants and animals in the wild, supported by activities in the classroom. Their investigations will include:

- exploration of different habitats;
- conditions needed for animals and plants to live;
- preferences shown by plants and animals for particular conditions;
- changes in environmental factors, and their effects on living things.

KEY IDEAS

- Living things live in a variety of places, which are called habitats.
- Living things are suited to the places in which they live.
- *Living things respond to changes in their environment.

(*Asterisks indicate ideas which will be developed more fully in later key stages.)

A LOOK AT habitats and environmental change

Living things can be found almost everywhere on the Earth, on land, sea or in the air. The places in which organisms live, such as a pond, a wood or a rockpool, are called habitats. Each habitat has its own particular set of conditions, for example of light, temperature, water, oxygen, and nutrients.

The kinds of animals and plants found in a rockpool differ from those found in a wood because animals and plants have features which suit them to a particular type of habitat – for example, the gills of fish which allow them to breathe under water but not on land.

The environment in which an organism lives consists of not only the physical conditions of its habitat but also the other living things with which it comes into contact. All living things can sense their environment and react to changes in it. Animals have some or all of the obvious senses (smell, hearing, taste, sight, touch). A deer, for example, will run away very quickly if it hears an unusual sound. A snail will retreat into its shell if it senses unusual conditions. Although most plants have no clearly visible senses, they all react to changes in the environment; for example, most of them grow towards the light.

How living things react to changes in their environment is important to their survival. This may be shown dramatically. For example, if a normally warm environment suddenly turns cold, some of the animals and plants will die; but those which can put up with low temperatures or move to a warmer place will survive. Other changes in the environment affect living things, but not so dramatically. For example, the growth cycles of plants and the behaviour of animals are influenced by seasonal changes.

3.1

Finding out children's ideas

STARTER ACTIVITIES

1 Where do plants and animals live?

A number of approaches to this activity can be used.

a Places where plants and animals might live

Start with a class brainstorming activity in response to the question:

Q *In what sorts of places do you think animals and plants might live?*

Encourage children to list as many different sorts of place as possible.

b Which animals and plants live in particular types of places?

Ask:

Q *What kinds of plants and animals do you think live*
- *in the air;*
- *in water;*
- *on land;*
- *under the ground?*

Use the examples of places suggested by the children during the brainstorming activity to ask more specifically:

Q *What kinds of animals and plants do you think live in (for example) a pond, a wood, a wall, the soil, a rockpool?*

Children can choose a place and make lists or drawings of the animals and plants they think might be found there.

c Where do particular animals and/or plants live?

Make lists of animals and plants, such as:

- cat, dog, rabbit, woodlouse, snail, stick insect, worm, caterpillar;
- daisy, dandelion, daffodil, spider plant, oak tree, pine tree, Canadian pondweed, reedmace (commonly but mistakenly called 'bulrush').

Divide the list into two groups, such as 'domestic animals and plants' and 'wild animals and plants'. Ask the children to choose one from each group, but do not tell them how the groups you have chosen are divided, as this will direct their thoughts too strongly.

Ask the children:

Q *Will you draw each of the animals or plants in what you think is the best place for it to live?*
Why do you think this is the best place for each of them to live?
Do you think either of them could live anywhere else?
What other sorts of places might either of them live in?

2 What do plants and animals need to live?

Why a plant or animal lives in a particular place depends on its being able to get all the things it needs to live. This activity is to find out what children think plants and animals need.

Children may 'adopt' a plant or animal in a local environment. They should observe it carefully and make an annotated drawing in response to the questions:

Q *What do you think the plant/animal needs to live?*
Where do you think it gets these things from?

Animals and plants kept in the classroom will also help to focus children's attention on the needs of organisms. Ask:

Q *What do you think needs to be done to look after this plant/animal properly?*
How do you think the plant/animal would get what it needed if it lived in the wild?

! FOLLOW SCHOOL OR LEA RULES ABOUT SUPERVISION.
CHECK YOUR SCHOOL'S POLICY ON VISITS

3 Changes in habitats

The changes that occur in habitats are very complex, so it is best to focus on one aspect at a time. It must nevertheless be remembered that all the aspects are closely related.

FOLLOW SCHOOL OR LEA RULES ABOUT SUPERVISION. CHECK YOUR SCHOOL'S POLICY ON VISITS

Visit a local habitat. Each child, or group of children, should select an area for observation and study. Older children may draw a map of the area, but each child or group should mark the area in some way so that it can be found again later.

After visiting a habitat, ask the children to draw a sequence of annotated diagrams in response to one or both of the questions:

Q *What do you think this place is like in spring, summer, autumn and winter?*
What do you think this place is like in the morning, afternoon and night?

In their drawings children are likely to include changes in both the environmental features (such as wind, rain or sunlight) and the animals and plants (for example, trees without leaves) in the habitat. Help the children to think about these different aspects by asking questions about environmental changes:

Q *When do you think this place is hot/warm/cold? What makes you say that?*
When do you think this place is dry/wet? Why do you think that?

You could also ask about changes in the plants and animals:

Q *What is different about the plants and animals here at different times of the year?*
Do all the plants and animals live here all the year?
What do you think happens to them?
Is there anything different about the plants and animals here at different times of the day? Why do you think that?

4 Animals and plants in a habitat

During a visit to a habitat children will see some of the plants and animals that live there. Ask them to draw an annotated picture of the habitat showing some of the plants and animals in response to the question:

Q *Why do you think these plants and animals live here?*

Discuss the children's drawings and ask:

Q *Do you think this is a good place for these plants and animals to live? Do you think any other plants and animals could live here?*
Can you think of plants and animals that could not live in this place? Why not?
Why do you think these plants and animals live here?

Discussing these questions provides an insight into children's understanding of the environmental influences on a habitat and the kinds of organisms that could live in it.

! FOLLOW SCHOOL OR LEA RULES ABOUT SUPERVISION.
CHECK YOUR SCHOOL'S POLICY ON VISITS

5 A selected plant in its habitat

Each child or group of children could select a plant from a habitat and produce a series of annotated drawings.

Q *Can you draw what the plant looks like at different times of the year? What do you think it looks like at different times of the day – morning, afternoon, night?*

Discussion of the drawings will help to reveal children's ideas. It may also encourage them to consider not only changes in the plant, but also accompanying changes in the habitat.

Other questions will help to reveal children's ideas about the suitability of the habitat for their selected plant.

Q *Do you think this is a good place for this plant to live? Why?*
Does the plant have anything that makes it easy for it to live in this place? Why do you think it helps?

! CHILDREN MAY NEED TO BE SUPERVISED.
CHECK YOUR SCHOOL'S POLICY ON VISITS

!

FOLLOW SCHOOL OR LEA RULES ABOUT SUPERVISION.
CHECK YOUR SCHOOL'S POLICY ON VISITS

6 A selected animal in its habitat

As with the selected plant, ask the children to produce a series of drawings of an animal in the habitat.

Q *Can you draw what the animal looks like at different times of the year?*
What do you think it looks like at different times of the day – morning, afternoon, night?

Other questions will help to reveal children's ideas about

- the behaviour of the animal:

Q *What do you think the animal does in spring, summer, autumn, winter? Why do you think it does this?*
What do you think this animal does in the morning, afternoon, night?

- the suitability of the habitat for the selected animal:

Q *Do you think this is a good place for this animal to live? Why do you think this is so?*
Does this animal have anything that makes it easy for it to live in this place? Why do you think it helps?

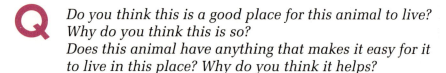

Children's ideas

Where do plants and animals live?

Most children can give examples of where plants and animals might live. The number and variety of places suggested tends to increase with the age of the children. When asked where the best place is for something to live, most children identify appropriate situations, as this example shows.

I think that this is a good surrounding because it is the normal surrounding for a snail and there is plenty on things for it to climb on
Soil
wood
Brick
carrots
worm
snail

Explanations of why an animal or a plant lives in a particular place often only reinforce the children's initial observations.

> *Worms live under the soil because it's dark and because worms like it dark.*
>
> *A stick insect could go on a tree 'cos it could hide from things and animals couldn't reach it.*

What do plants and animals need to live?

Plants

The most common requirements mentioned are water, soil and sunlight. Few young children give all three. Although 'soil' is not written down in this drawing it clearly shows the plants growing in soil.

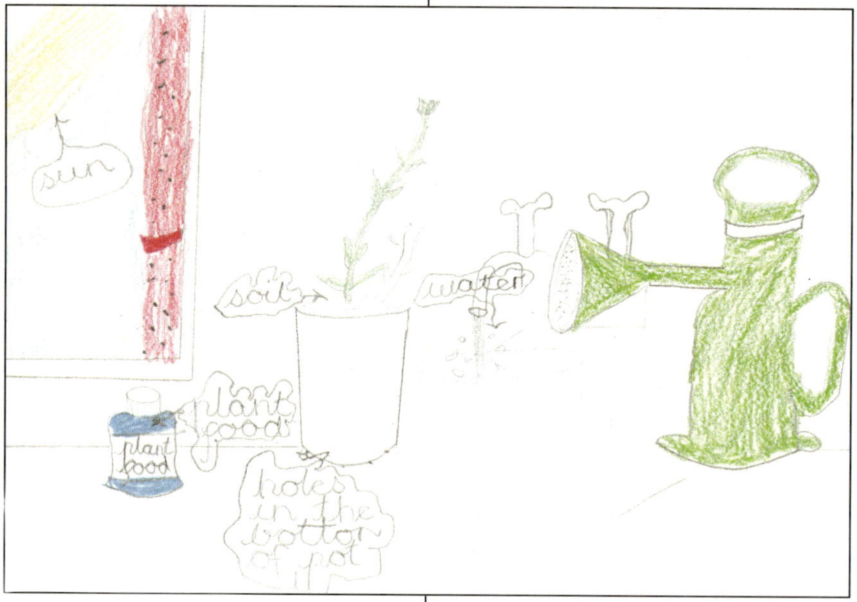

Some children are able to make the distinction between the light and warmth from the Sun; with older children, 'light' is a more common response than 'Sun'.

The youngest children omit 'air' or 'plant food' or 'drainage', and only a minority of older children include these items in their response.

Whilst 'soil' is nearly always given as a requirement for plants it is not often seen as a source of nutrients. Some children suggest that plants get their 'food' from the soil through their roots. However, these responses do not seem to recognize that plants 'make their own food'.

> *The plant will need leaves to get air, it will need roots to collect food and water and a stem to carry the food to the flower.*

Animals

Children's responses as to what animals require to live often reflect those given for plants. The requirements given tend to be more limited, with food being the most important. This may suggest that children recognize one of the real distinctions between plants and animals – that animals need an external food source.

The first example gives the basic requirements. Young children often include the Sun as a 'need'.

best place to live is in the grass
snail needs
leaves
rain
sun
grass

This drawing is more specific about the food source and introduces the idea that animals need protection from other animals.

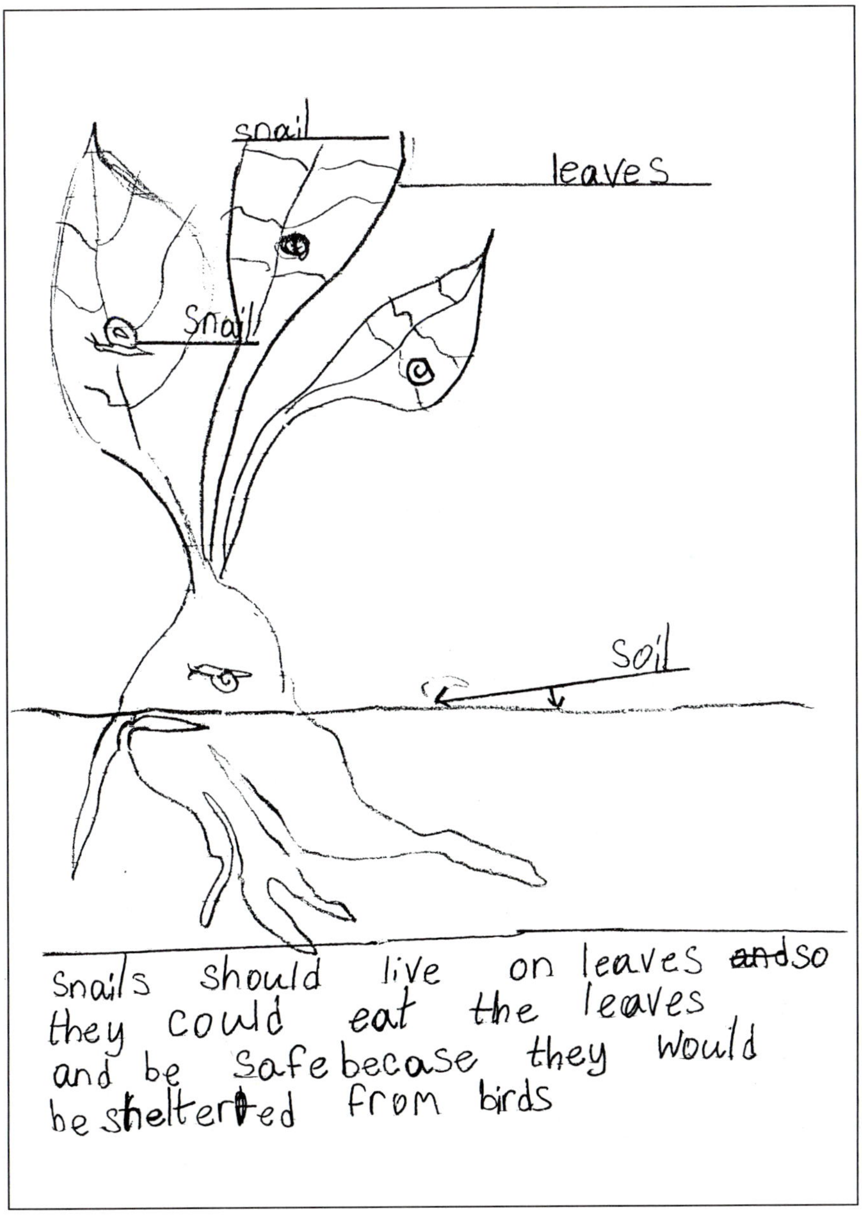

snail
leaves
snail
soil
Snails should live on leaves ~~and~~so they could eat the leaves and be safe becase they would be sheltered from birds

3.1

Changes in habitats

Most children are aware of seasonal changes in an area. Their responses show the major environmental changes. The importance of the Sun in relation to seasonal change is very evident. Winter pictures portray snow but rarely include the Sun. In other seasons the Sun is a constant feature. In summer it is often central, large and bright, in spring it is clearly visible and in autumn it is either absent or accompanied by clouds or rain.

Plants and environmental changes

Changes in leaf colour, and the fall of leaves, are noticed by almost all children.

In Autumn leaves fall from the trees. the leaves are yellow brown orange and red leaves.

In contrast, children rarely refer to other changes, such as the appearance of flowers, fruits and seeds.

A popular idea among children of all ages is that plants die during the winter. Children make little distinction between annual and perennial plants, often referring to plants or parts of plants as 'dead'. Their meaning of 'dead' in this case could be questioned further.

Nearly all children recognize that plants change during the year. However, the sequence on the right is one of the few examples in which children directly relate the changes in a plant to the environmental changes.

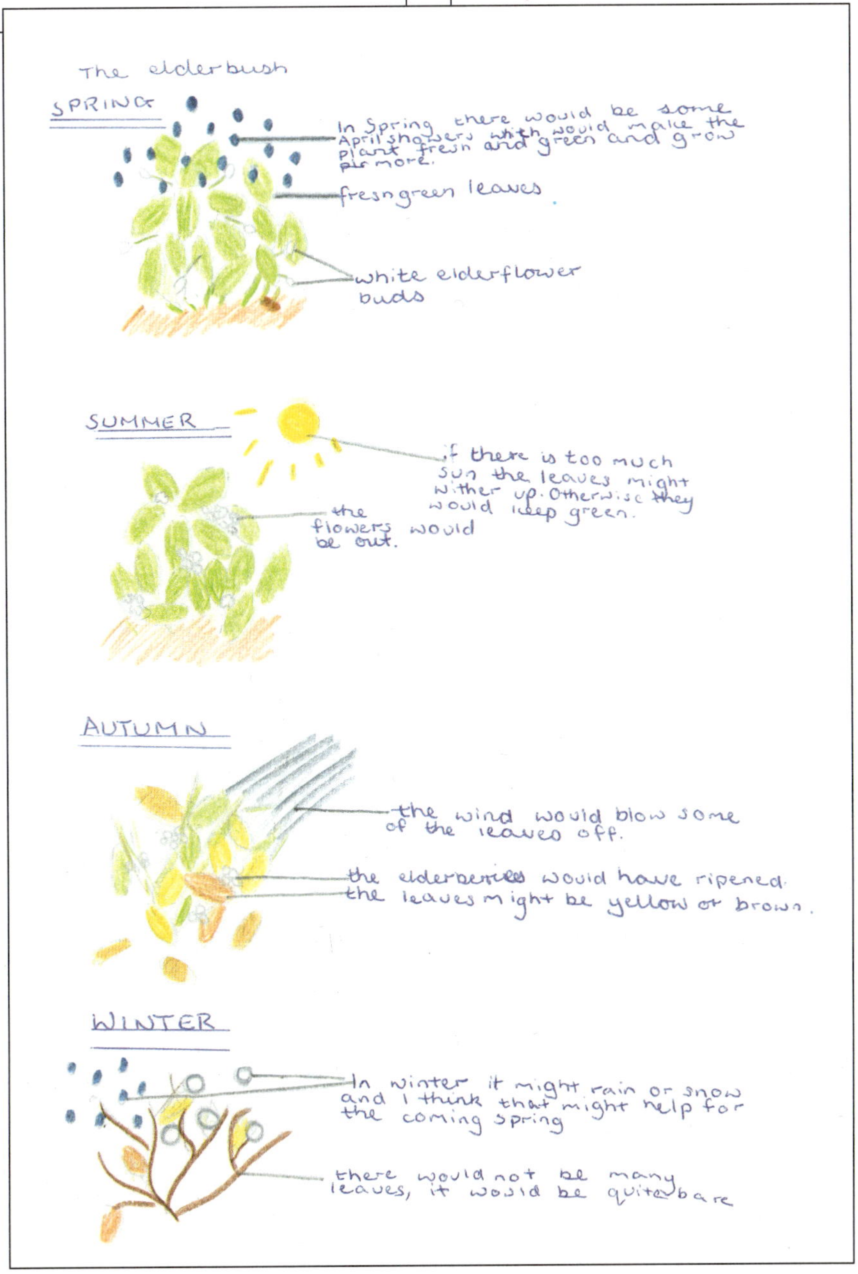
The elderbush
SPRING
In Spring there would be some April showers which would make the plant fresh and green and grow more.
fresh green leaves
white elderflower buds
SUMMER
if there is too much sun the leaves might wither up. Otherwise they would keep green.
the flowers would be out.
AUTUMN
the wind would blow some of the leaves off.
the elderberries would have ripened.
the leaves might be yellow or brown.
WINTER
In winter it might rain or snow and I think that might help for the coming spring
there would not be many leaves, it would be quite bare

Animals and environmental changes

Many children express ideas about the impact of different seasons on the animals found in their habitat.

In this example the behaviour of birds is highlighted and shows clear awareness of migration.

Autumn
It is now autumn
and the leaves are turning
red ready fall.
The blackbird
is fully grown
ready to migrate
The strip of grass
(middle) bottom has changed
colour
Winter
It is winter
everything is white
the bird has migrated
and their are no leaves
on the trees

Children's drawings and written accounts, especially of birds, often include descriptions of the role of the parents in the development of the young. These accounts demonstrate awareness of the importance of nest building, and of feeding and nurturing the young until they are able to fend for themselves. Interestingly, children's descriptions of all animals often include parallels with their own experience of development, emphasizing the significant role of training and anticipation of future independence.

This account of what a hedgehog does during the year is a good example. This child, along with many others, also refers to a long period of hibernation.

A hedgehog

Winter
In the winter the hedgehog will be hibetnating under a bush. He will have a supply of food near by to eat while he his hibernating.

Spring
In spring the hedgehog will wake up to go and find a wife then he will bring his wife home and they will have four or five babys

Summer
In Summer the hedgehogs will teach the babies how to get food and to look after themselfs Then they will leaves them and they will live of there own.

Autumn
In Autumn the hedgehogs will settle down for there hibernation and hang their stockings up for father hedgehog

In the responses children make, evidence of other ideas occurs from time to time. For example, this piece of writing indicates children's ability to make interpretations based on their observations. Of particular note here is the reference to the shape of the tree helping 'to try and pick up all the sun', suggesting some realization that organisms can adapt.

In our little area there was a big tree with ivy clinging to it, just a few inches away there was a small tree that was growing Next to that there was a stump of a tree that had either cut down or fallen down with a thick covering of ivy. Around the edge of the area bluebells were growing along with the high grass In the heart of the area little shrubs were growing just getting past being choked by the brambles. The biggest tree had its branches in a sort of umbrella shape propably to try and shade th pick up all the sun The trees trunk grows out to the left making way for little creatures to make their nest in the ivy covering it On the stump going out to the left is the remains of an ants nest maybe still some living there but I didn't see any crawling round there was a lot of spiders webs and I even saw one spider on its web. There was the odd dandilion and I even saw a rat hole covered in grass.

Helping children to develop their ideas

The charts on the following pages show how you can help children to develop their ideas from starting points which have given rise to different ideas.

The centre rectangles contain starter questions.

The surrounding 'thought bubbles' contain the sorts of ideas expressed by children.

The further ring of rectangles contains questions posed by teachers in response to the ideas expressed by the children. These questions are meant to prompt children to think about their ideas.

The outer ovals indicate ways in which the children might respond to the teacher's questions.

Some of the shapes have been left blank, as a sign that other ideas may be encountered and other ways of helping children to develop their ideas may be tried.

1 Where do animals and plants live?

The activities suggested are complementary and not meant as alternatives.

a Go on safari!

The idea of this safari is *not* to collect as many plants and animals as possible, but to record where things live. Identify a particular area, preferably with several different parts to it such as the school grounds, a neighbouring street, a park. Depending on the age of the pupils, a map of the area could be drawn up and used.

FOLLOW SCHOOL OR LEA RULES ABOUT SUPERVISION.
CHECK YOUR SCHOOL'S POLICY ON VISITS

3.1

Helping children to develop their ideas about habitats and environmental change

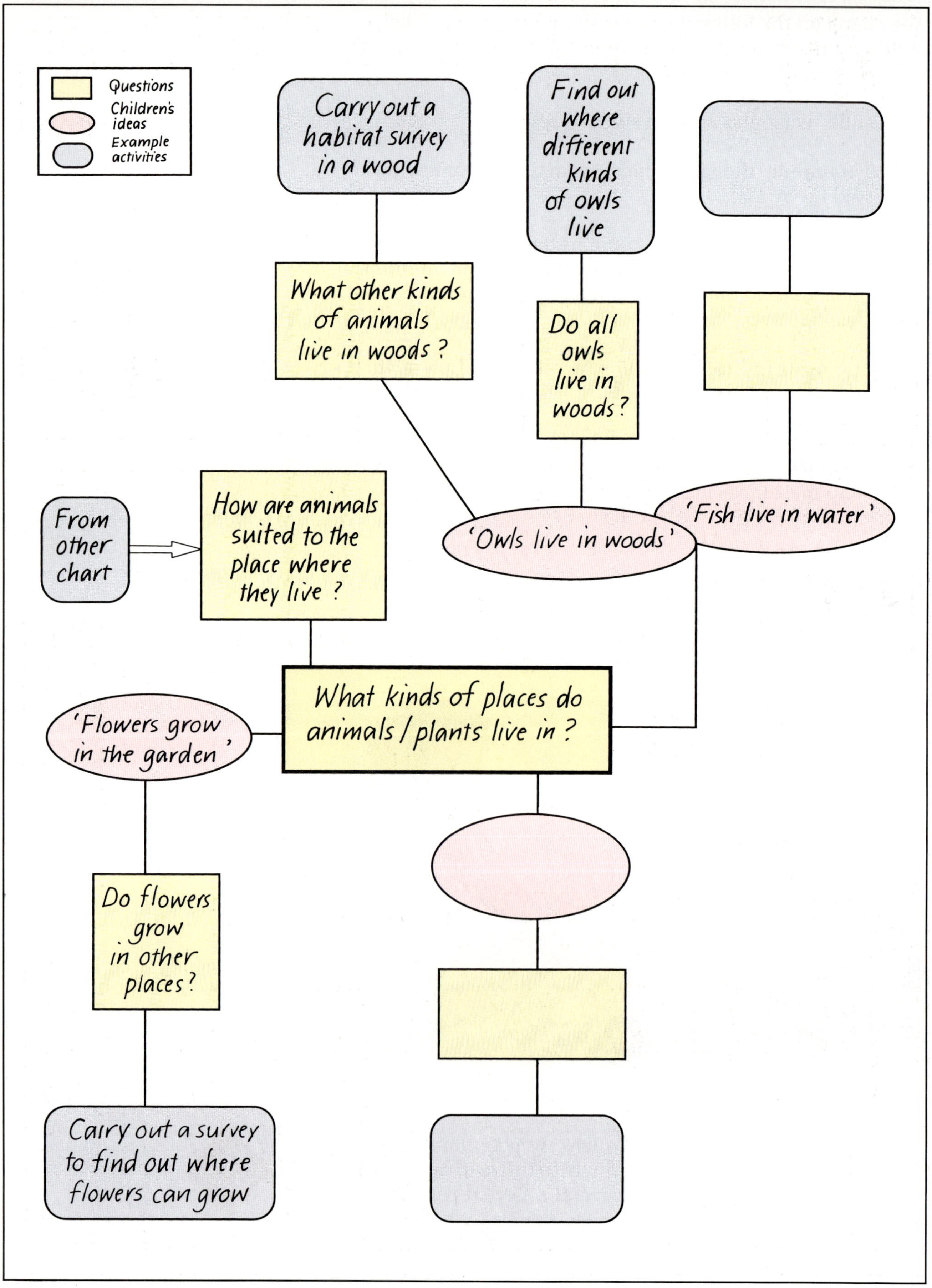
Questions
Children's ideas
Example activities
Carry out a habitat survey in a wood
Find out where different kinds of owls live
What other kinds of animals live in woods?
Do all owls live in woods?
From other chart
How are animals suited to the place where they live?
'Owls live in woods'
'Fish live in water'
What kinds of places do animals/plants live in?
'Flowers grow in the garden'
Do flowers grow in other places?
Carry out a survey to find out where flowers can grow

Questions
Children's ideas
Example activities

How do living things interact with their environment?

How are animals suited to the place where they live?

Does any plant come up in the same place next year?

Look at anything left underground. Visit garden centre or use catalogues. What do 'annual' and 'perennial' mean?

'Plants die in winter'

Is any part of the 'dead' plant left underground?

'Their feet help them in walking on marshy ground'

How do other animals' feet help them?

Observation of feet of different birds and animals backed up by secondary sources seeing how they may differ according to habitat

'They can get what they need'

What do plants/animals need?

Find out the needs of plants and animals

What is different about plants at different times of the year?

'Leaves die off in winter'

'They blend in with their surroundings'

How do animals blend in?

Study of camouflage, how it's achieved, reasons why it's necessary

Do all plants lose their leaves?

Observe different plants in winter. Classify as deciduous or evergreen.

To other chart

'Animals die in winter'

What kinds of animals die?

Use of secondary sources to see how animals can survive winter

Do any birds arrive here for winter?

Observance of the kinds of birds that migrate. Discussions of reasons why birds might migrate

'Birds fly away'

Do all birds fly away?

'Hedgehogs hibernate'

Which other animals hibernate?

Study of hibernation. Discussion about why it might occur

What is different about animals at different times of the year?

'Some animals grow different coats'

Use of secondary sources to see how a winter coat can provide camouflage

How does a different coat help?

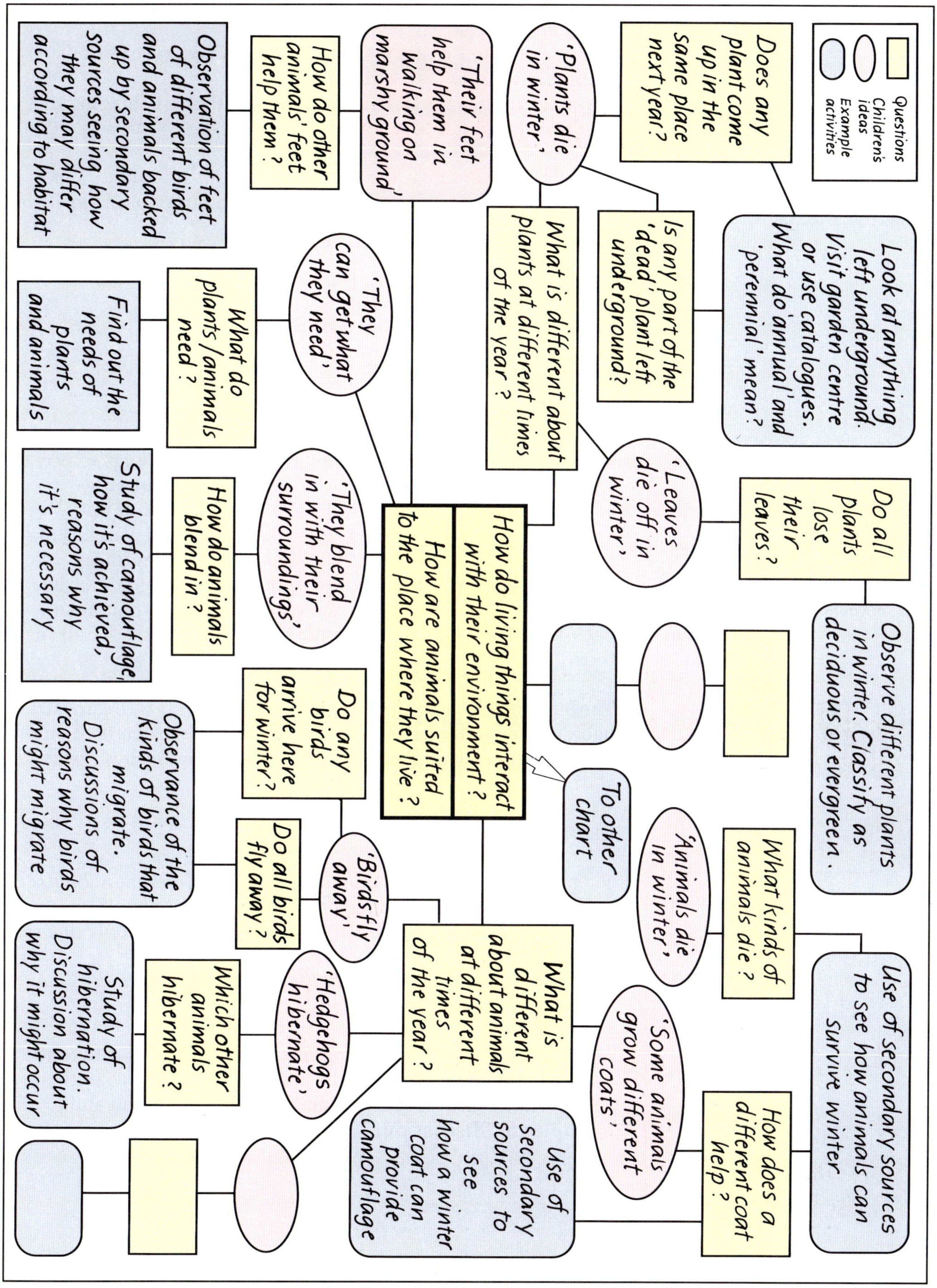

3.1

t LIVING THINGS LIVE IN A VARIETY OF PLACES

Ask the children to:

- identify and record as many different places as possible where they find animals or plants living;
- find the most unusual place where they can discover a living thing;
- if they cannot remember the proper names, record finds simply as 'plant' or 'animal';
- record the results of the safari on a wall chart showing the places in which they found living things.

AT 1 OBSERVING

To extend the activity, the children can return to particular places on their safari and, through careful observation and discussion, consider questions such as:

Q *What living things live here?*
Why do they live here?
How did they get to this place?
What do the things living here need?

b Use of secondary sources

Books, videos, and discussion with people with some expert knowledge (often other children) can extend children's appreciation of the variety of places in which plants and animals can be found living. The results of these searches may be brought together on a big wall chart which identifies different types of habitat where living things are found. The charts may contain not only the types of habitats that have been identified, but also examples of the organisms found in them.

The search may take a broad sweep (land habitats, freshwater habitats, saltwater habitats) or focus on different parts of one habitat such as woodland (what lives in trees, bushes, rocks, soil).

AT 1 COMMUNICATING

Discuss:

Q *What plants and animals live in the different habitats?*
Can any of them live in more than one habitat?
Why do you think some living things live in only one sort of place?
Is there anything about them that helps them live in a particular place?

pb

Habitats and *More about habitats* give examples of different habitats and some of the plants and animals that live in them. These can be used to provide additional information and examples for discussion.

c Habitat collage

Prepare with the children a large drawing of a particular habitat such as a wood, a pond, or a rocky shore.

Ask the children to:

- find out what different plants and animals might live in such a place;
- draw, or collect from magazines, pictures of the plants and animals;
- mount the pictures of plants and animals on the large drawing where each one of them would most likely be found.

Discuss the children's reasons for their distribution of the plants and animals. This activity could be carried out together with the habitat survey described on page 51.

pb

Habitats could be used as a starting point for this activity and provides material on which to base discussions. The pupils' book gives the children a habitat to fill with living things. You could alternatively give them a large blank sheet of paper and ask them to start by designing the habitat. Children could choose from the cards given on the copiable sheets on pages 56-59. In some cases they might want to write on the card the number of specimens of a particular creature they want to include.

2 What do plants and animals need to live?

!

Investigative work with living things has ethical and legal obligations, so choose practical investigations with care. The collection of plants and animals from the wild is severely restricted – see *Animals and plants in schools: legal aspects* (DES Administrative Memorandum 3/90).

a What do plants need to live?

AT 1 GENERAL

A class discussion of this question will reveal many ideas of what might be investigated. These ideas can then be used to set up fair tests – some children might be challenged to design tests for themselves. (See also *Living Processes*.)

e

Different types of seeds can be used, such as mustard, cress, beans, peas and mung beans. (Avoid red kidney beans, the skins of which are toxic until cooked.)

t LIVING THINGS REQUIRE CERTAIN CONDITIONS

Cress seeds generally germinate very reliably and will produce results in days. The test might be run with:

- one dish/jar in the light, for example on a windowsill;
- one in the dark, for example in a cupboard;
- one in a cold place, for example a refrigerator;
- one in the light, but with the cotton wool left dry.

It is important that the children are fully involved in the design of tests such as this, and that they are satisfied that it is fair. Ask:

Q

Which factors are you going to keep the same?
Which factor is going to be changed?
How are you going to record the results? How often?
What do you think is going to happen?
Which do you think will be the best conditions for these plants?
What is needed for the seeds to start growing?
What is needed for the new plants to keep growing?
Do the seeds and the new plants need the same conditions?

Further work might involve growing a variety of plants in different situations, both indoors and outdoors, and monitoring their growth by both careful observation and measurement.

b What conditions do animals prefer?

!

Investigations in which animals might be harmed must be avoided, but some investigations can be carried out. For example:

t — WOODLICE TEND TO PREFER DARK, MOIST PLACES

Q *What conditions do woodlice prefer?*

This question might be investigated by:

i Creating a 'mini-habitat'

e

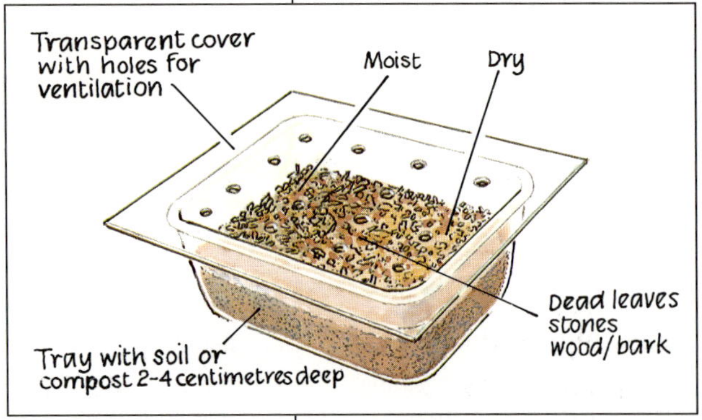

Put 30 woodlice in a tray as shown here. Then, at intervals during each day for a week, look for the place where most woodlice are found. Keep a class log book to record where the woodlice are found. You will need to keep the damp area moist by spraying it with water, and ensure that at least one area has a food supply. You also need to keep at least part of it dark.

Ensure that the woodlice are returned to the habitat from which they came after the investigation is finished.

ii Using choice chambers

e

This equipment enables investigators to compare responses to different conditions, such as wet/dry, warm/cold, light/dark; and also food preferences. (You could use a commercial choice chamber.)

A number of woodlice are put into the chamber at the centre and left for a short while (5 minutes, or possibly more). At the end of the time the number of woodlice in each part of the chamber is counted and recorded.

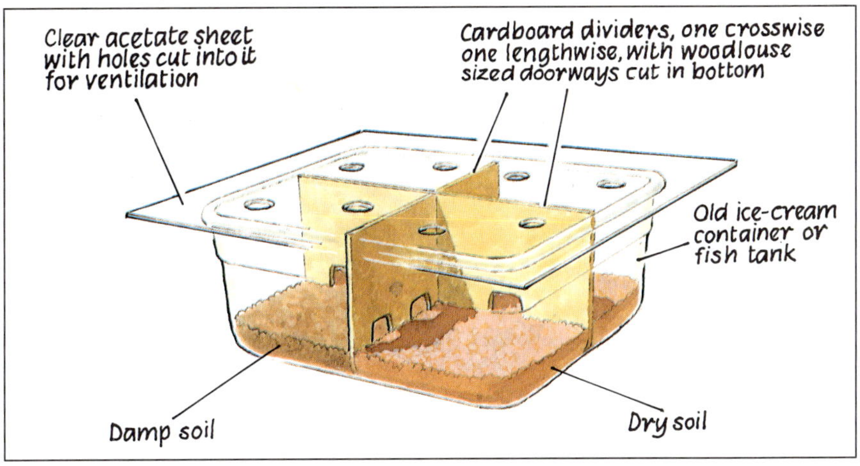

Alternatively, children could record the numbers at intervals for a period of, say, 5 to 10 minutes, and draw up a table – perhaps on the lines of the one shown here.

These results could then be presented as a bar chart or graph.

AT 1 INTERPRETING RESULTS AND FINDINGS

Time from start	Number of woodlice in dark	Number of woodlice in light
0 minutes (start)		
1 minute		
2 minutes		

Similar investigations can be carried out with other 'minibeasts', such as snails and earthworms.

Much development of ideas about animals' requirements depends on discussion based on related experiences. These include observations made of animals in their natural habitat, and the needs of animals that are normally taken into consideration while caring for them.

c Caring for living things

Encourage children to care for living things actively.

Before keeping animals in classrooms, seek guidance from the RSPCA publications 'Animals in schools' and 'Small mammals in schools'. Only obtain animals from reputable suppliers.

i In the classroom

Give children the opportunity to carry out routine care and maintenance of plants and animals. Encourage them to:

- identify the needs of the organism;

t

LIVING THINGS HAVE SPECIFIC REQUIREMENTS

!

CHILDREN MUST WASH THEIR HANDS BEFORE AND AFTER HANDLING ANIMALS.
WASH ANIMAL BITES AND SCRATCHES CAREFULLY, AND CONSIDER THE NEED FOR MEDICAL ADVICE

- meet those needs through appropriate action;
- observe and record the appearance or behaviour of the plant/animal;
- consider how these needs are met for plants/animals in the wild.

Keep some form of log book – class, group or individual.

Discuss the comments regularly, and consider any patterns both in the care of the plant/animal and in its appearance or behaviour. Investigate:

Q *How much water does the plant/animal use in a day/week?*
Does the mass of the animal/plant change?

ii In the environment

The care of animals and plants also involves consideration of wildlife.

Arrange a visit to a zoo, nature reserve, conservation area or bird sanctuary. Then ask:

!

CHECK YOUR SCHOOL'S POLICY ON VISITS

Q *How are the plants and animals cared for?*

Consider the arguments for and against zoos/nature reserves.

Use secondary source material to extend the range of examples the children can consider.

Encourage children to get involved with wildlife projects practically – for example, by creating a nature area at the school and looking after it themselves.

(The construction of a nature area should not be undertaken lightly – it is a major, time-consuming project which needs thorough planning, the approval of the headteacher, governors, and caretaker, and the support of parents and local community. You will need a management plan – for instance, when will the grass be cut, and by whom? However, such a project gives a habitat that can be visited easily and frequently and is well worth the effort.)

Discuss the issues involved in wildlife projects:

Q *Do you think it is important to look after wildlife? Why?*
If you were in the government what would you do to help look after wildlife?

More about habitats looks at Everglades in Florida where animals and plants are under pressure from development. Children can use this as a basis for discussion and as a starting point for further enquiry.

3 A habitat survey

When planning to investigate a habitat, take account of the time span of the survey. The habitat could be monitored for a day, a week, a month, or throughout the year. Longer investigations are likely to develop a better understanding. Each situation is different, and it may be that a combination of the possibilities, including visits to other areas, is most profitable.

The important points are that:

- the area should be easily accessible;
- it should be as safe as possible;
- at least two different habitats should be compared.

CHECK YOUR SCHOOL'S POLICY ON VISITS. BE ESPECIALLY CAREFUL ABOUT PONDS

(See 'Safety and the school pond' in *Primary science review*, summer 1988.)

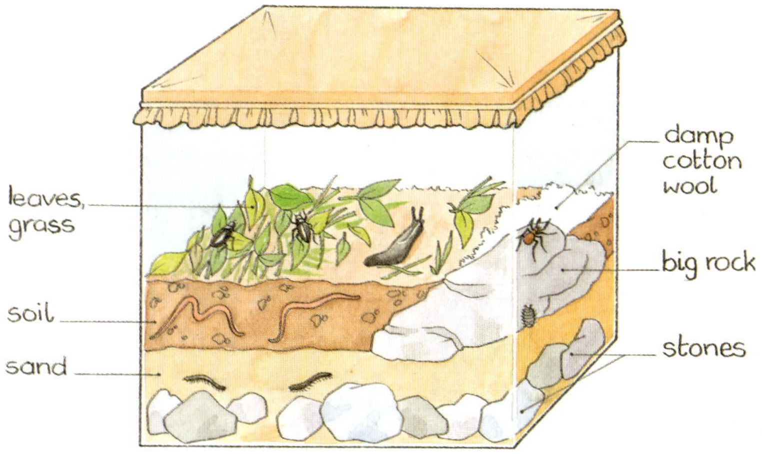

The activities suggested here should be based on studies of natural habitats if at all possible: a pond, wooded area, sand dune, rocky shore, meadow, heathland or hedgerow. When these are not easily accessible, alternatives can usually be found, such as a small area of rough grass, an overgrown flowerbed, a quiet part of the local churchyard.

The area does not have to be very large. A great deal can be discovered in areas of 2 by 1 metres, sometimes even less. Old walls can be very rich in animal and plant species. In addition, it is possible to create habitats both inside and outside, using various materials and containers. The basic requirements of soil, water and rocks can be assembled, and appropriate animals and plants introduced.

Other places which are suitable for study are what can be called 'micro-habitats', such as a rotting log, under stones, a compost heap, a tub of rainwater, or discarded roof guttering. In these very small areas a whole variety of life can be found and studied. (See also *The Variety of Life* and *Living Processes*.)

3.1

e

AT 1
OBSERVING
MEASURING
INTERPRETING RESULTS
AND FINDINGS
COMMUNICATING

a Environmental features

Children should measure and record features of the habitat such as:

- ◆ size (use standard or non-standard units);
- ◆ where it is in relation to other habitats, buildings, etc. (mark these on a map or sketch);
- ◆ whether it gets sunlight at certain times of day or is shaded;
- ◆ temperatures, which may be measured in different parts of the habitat and at different times of the day and year;
- ◆ some measure of how wet the habitat is (soil moisture meters can be obtained from garden centres);
- ◆ the materials – rock, wood, soil – that make up the habitat;
- ◆ acidity/alkalinity of the soil or water (garden soil testing kits may be used);
- ◆ wind strength and direction.

t

HABITATS DIFFER IN THEIR ENVIRONMENTAL FEATURES

Bar charts and graphs can be produced to show the changes in some of these environmental factors for a day, week, month or year.

b Living things in the habitat

t

LIVING THINGS TEND TO LIVE IN PARTICULAR TYPES OF HABITAT

As well as recording environmental features, types and numbers of creatures in the habitat should be recorded.

i Animals

AT 1
OBSERVING

One possible objective of this activity is to establish which animals are to be seen (not collected!) in the selected habitat at the beginning and towards the end of the period during which visits take place. Children could collect information about names of animals, the number of animals of the same species, where they were found and what they were doing. Animals could be included whether they are alive or dead.

Animal	How many seen	Where?	What were they doing?

It may be useful for children to summarize their information in a chart like this.

It may help to divide the class into groups so that each group is responsible for locating and identifying particular types of animals, such as:

- ◆ 'minibeasts' on the ground or under stones;
- ◆ flying animals including birds;
- ◆ larger ground-living animals (small mammals, frogs and toads);
- ◆ aquatic animals (if the habitat includes water).

ii Plants

Similarly, children could record the type and number of plants in the habitat, or estimate the fraction or percentage of the area covered by a plant species.

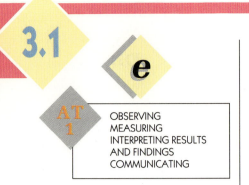

WARN CHILDREN ABOUT POISONOUS PLANTS – ESPECIALLY ATTRACTIVE FRUITS AND BERRIES. TEACH THEM NEVER TO TASTE ANY PART OF A PLANT UNLESS ABSOLUTELY CERTAIN THAT IT IS SAFE

Make this easier by helping the children to look at small areas of ground of a standard size (such as 0.5 by 0.5 metres). Simple wooden frames can be made to ease measurement – these are called quadrats. Hoops could also be used. Children can compare the number of plants in quadrats from different parts of the habitat and consider the question:

e

AT 1 MEASURING OBSERVING INTERPRETING RESULTS AND FINDINGS

Q *Does the number and type of plants change from one part of the habitat to another?*
What might be the cause of any differences?

Another way of comparing different parts of the habitat is to mark a line across a piece of ground from one side to the other. Note the plants (and animals) that can be seen at one end. Move a standard distance (say, 1 pace, 5 paces or 2 metres) and record the plants at that place. Move on and repeat the process until the other side is reached. At each place put a quadrat on the ground to mark out the area to be searched.

Both the plant and animal activities provide excellent opportunities for careful observation and recording. Visit the same habitat several times to enable children to consider the changes in the organisms they observe, including their range, number and appearance or behaviour.

AT 1 OBSERVING MEASURING

A computer database may be used for the recording and analysis of habitat survey information. Children could then do a search to find common features of plants and/or animals found in a particular location.

it

AT 1 COMMUNICATING

Discussion of the findings, which can be presented as wall charts and posters including bar charts, will give the children ample opportunity to respond to questions such as:

Q *Why do the animals and plants live where they do?*
What effect do you think the conditions have on them?
How are they suited to their environment?

Secondary sources providing information on the same kind of habitat and other habitats could help children extend their ideas and relate particular organisms to particular environments.

c Observing changes in a plant

AT 1 — OBSERVING, MEASURING, INTERPRETING RESULTS AND FINDINGS

It is very difficult to observe animals in the wild over an extended period, but it is quite easy to observe changes in plants.

This activity provides opportunities for measurement as well as observation, and the use of equipment such as a hand lens.

Encourage each child or group of children to select a plant which they can monitor over at least a week, or preferably longer. It is useful to mark the plant so that it can be easily found. Try to ensure that children consider a plant in which you would expect some perceptible changes to occur, such as wild flowers, shrubs or trees.

e

Ask the children to make a series of drawings of the plant during the course of their visits, showing the changes that occur. They may need to use a hand lens for close observation. The children could also look carefully at other plants of the same species so that they develop some awareness of individual variation within a species (see *The variety of life* teachers' guide, page 69).

The frequency with which drawings can usefully be made will depend on the nature and rate of the changes taking place. Often no more than four drawings spanning the period will provide an adequate record of change and prevent the task becoming tedious.

Children should also be asked to draw the changes which may occur during the life cycle of the plant. Encourage them by asking:

Q *How did the plant come to grow there? How did it start?*
At what time of the year do you think it may have started?
What did it look like right at the beginning?
How long do you think it has been growing?
Tell me about the buds/flowers/seed pods etc. What happens to them? What are they for?
Tell me what you think is going to happen to this plant.
If you looked in the same place next year, what would you find?

d Relating changes in plants and animals to the seasons

Explore through class discussion how far children can relate changes in plants and animals to seasonal changes.

t — LIVING THINGS CHANGE IN RESPONSE TO ENVIRONMENTAL CHANGES

Q *What changes did you notice in the plants?*
What changes did you notice in the animals?
If you went to the same place at another time of the year, what differences would you notice in the plants?
If you went to the same place at another time of the year, what differences would you notice in the animals?

This provides scope for recognizing patterns of behaviour.

pb

Habitats shows an example of a habitat at different times of the year. Children could discuss the changes that occur and compare them with their own observations.

More about habitats shows how one person recorded changes by making careful observations and drawings of plants and animals throughout a year.

4 Plant and animal adaptation

The activities in this section ask children to think about the features of plants and animals that help them in their environment. This is not an easy matter, and perhaps requires a separate activity.

Use a combination of first-hand observation and secondary source material.

Ask children to collect information on particular animal features such as:

t — LIVING THINGS HAVE FEATURES WHICH ARE HELPFUL TO THEM IN THEIR HABITAT

- birds' beaks;
- positions of eyes;
- colouring and camouflage;
- well developed senses, such as hearing and smell.

pb

There are some suitable pictures in *Different plants and animals* and *More about different plants and animals.*

Discuss such features and ask:

t — SOME FEATURES CAN BE A HINDRANCE IN THE WRONG HABITAT

Q *How do you think this (e.g.) shape of beak helps the creature in its environment?*
Do you think it has any disadvantages?

It is more difficult to show plant adaptations, but it is worth looking at, for example:

- desert plants such as cacti;
- how various flowers are pollinated.

pb

More about habitats gives examples of plants and animals living in harsh conditions. Their adaptations can be discussed.

3.1 Design a habitat 1: habitats

tree

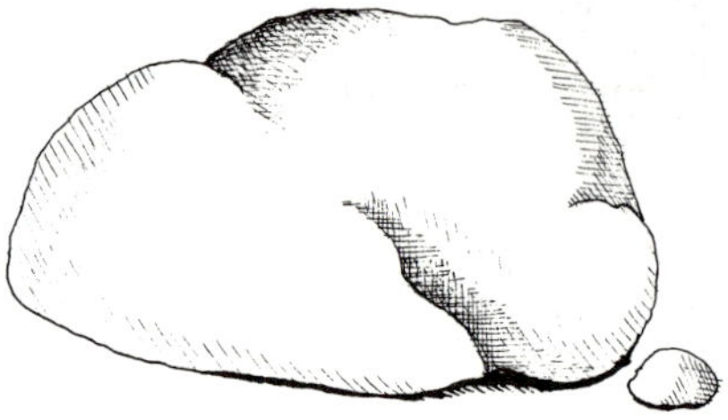

rock

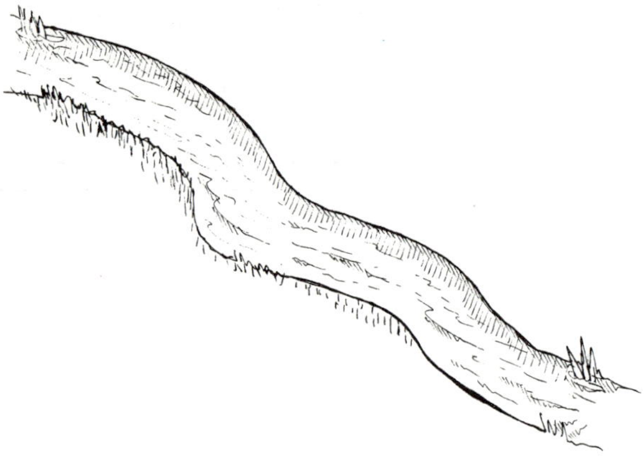

stream

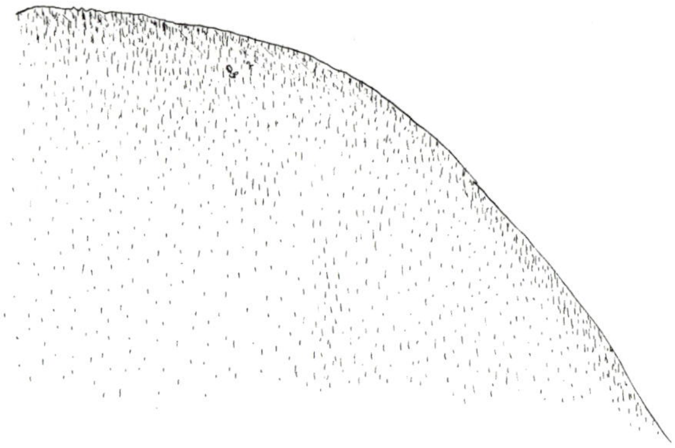

hillside

shrub

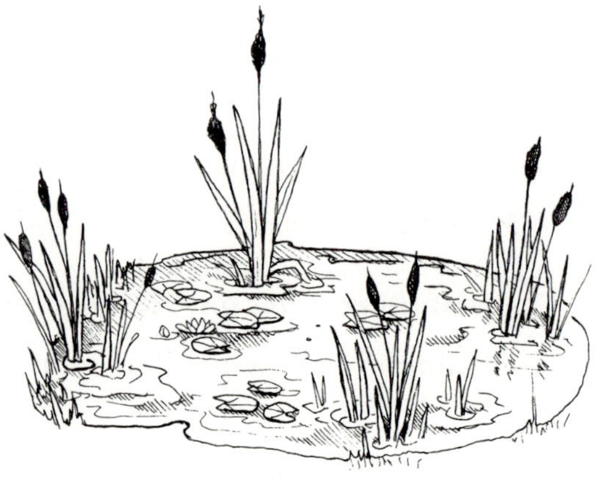

pond

Design a habitat 2: plants and fungi

3.1

oak tree

willow

douglas fir

blackberries

daisies

dandelion

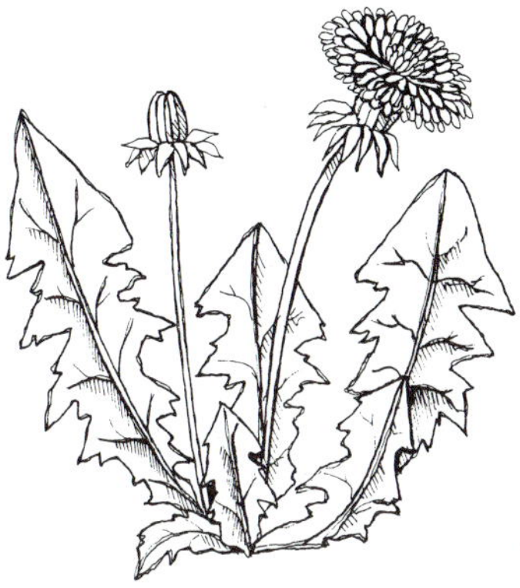

clover

nettles

marsh marigolds

poppies

rushes

mushrooms

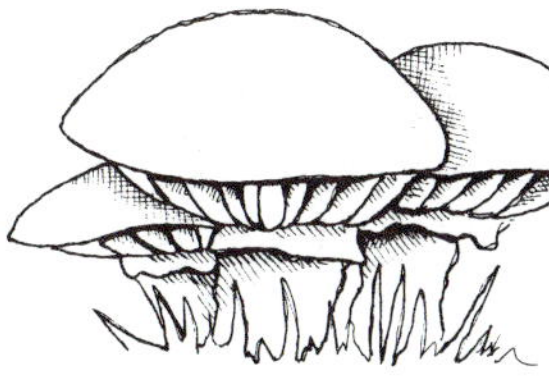

3.1 Design a habitat 3: small animals

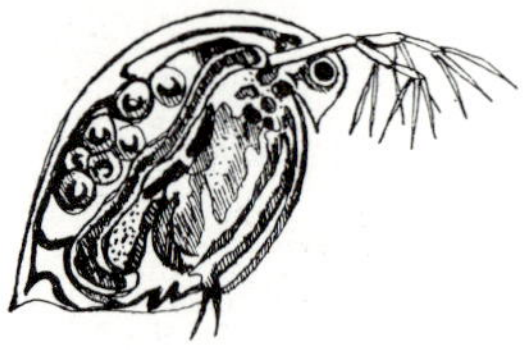
waterflea

aphids

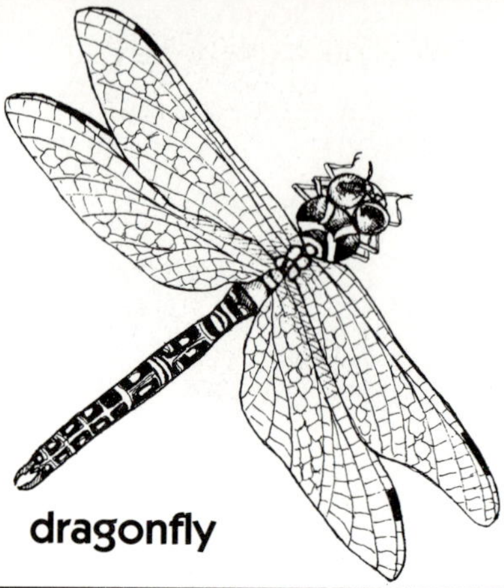
dragonfly

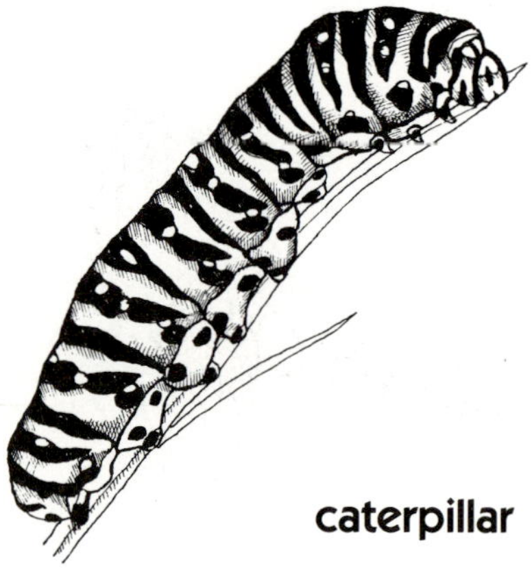
caterpillar

butterfly

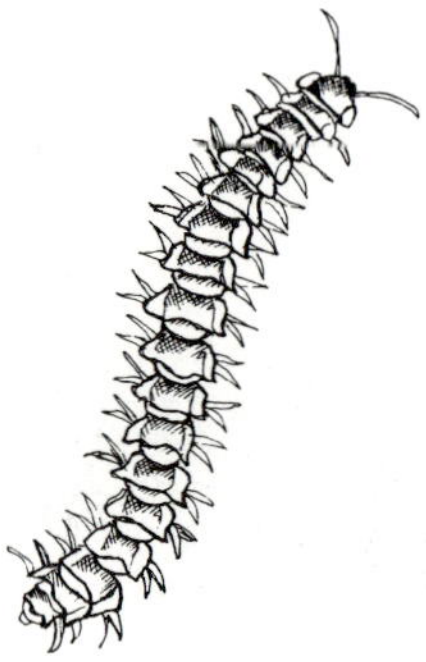
millipede

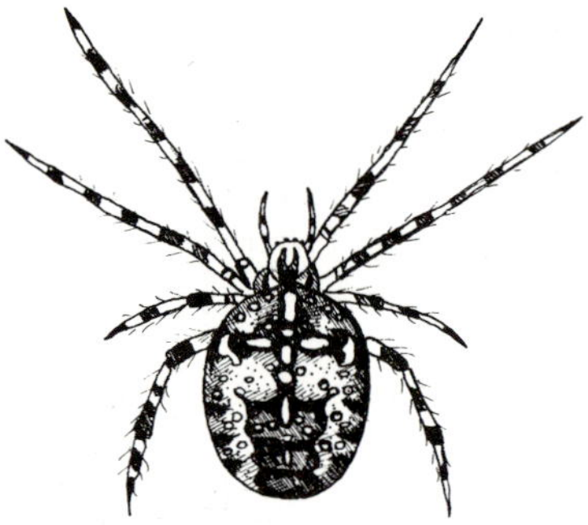
spider

worm
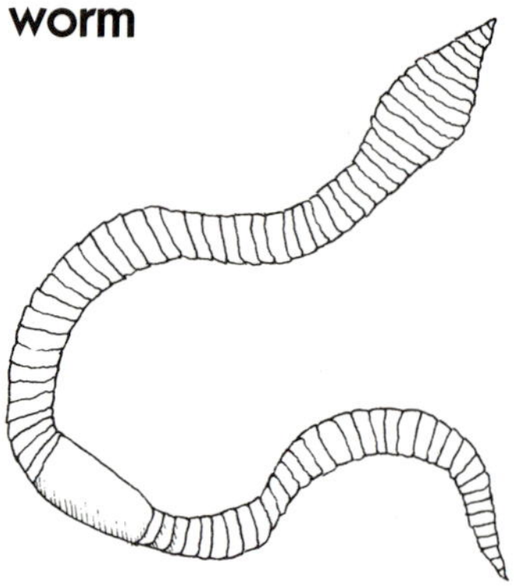

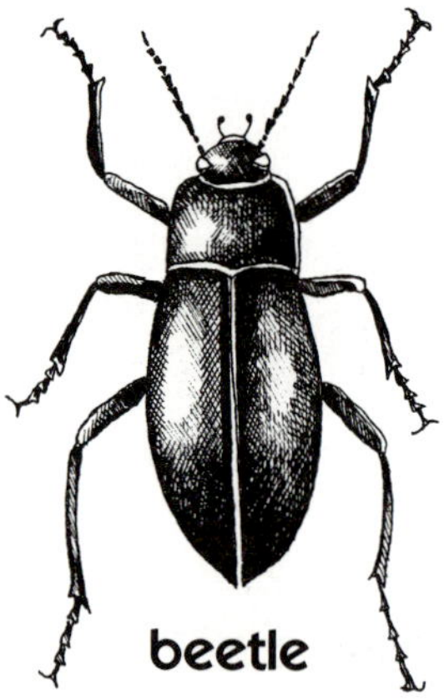
beetle

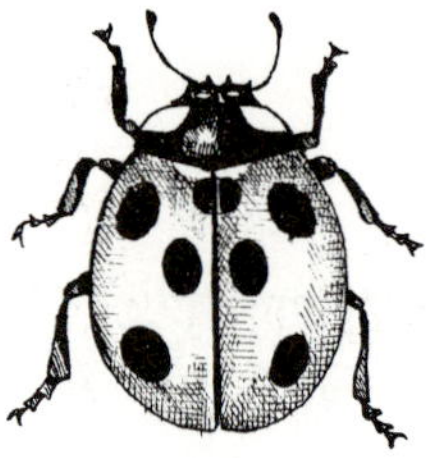
ladybird

earwig

fly

Design a habitat 4: large animals

3.1

tawny owl

rabbit

sparrowhawk

pheasant

fox

blackbird

sparrow

mouse

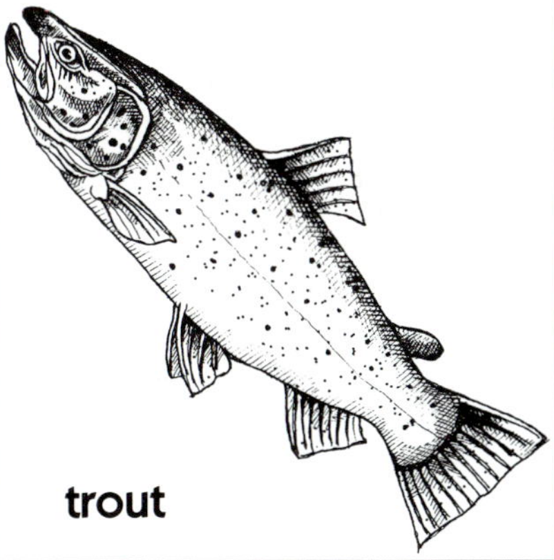

trout

children

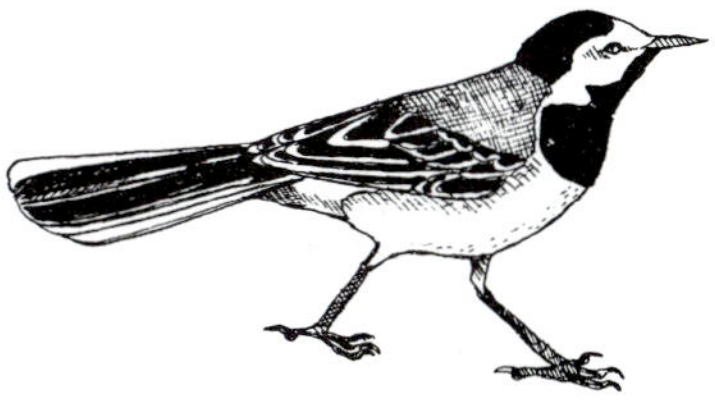

pied wagtail

nuthatch

3.2

Feeding relationships between c

AREAS FOR INVESTIGATION

- Ways in which animals and plants get their food.
- Ways in which animals and plants interact with each other.

The activities suggested in this theme could form part of the work described in 'Habitats and environmental change' (page 28). See also *Living Processes.*

KEY IDEAS

- Living things need certain conditions to stay alive.
- Plants are the ultimate source of food for all living things.
- *Living things interact with each other in various ways, including competition for resources.

(* Asterisks indicate ideas which will be developed more fully in later key stages)

A LOOK AT feeding relationships between organisms

All living things need food, oxygen, water and shelter so that they can survive in their environment. Plants also need light and carbon dioxide.

Food is the source of energy that organisms need to live. It also provides them with the raw materials that they need for growing.

Plants make their own food when carbon dioxide reacts with water in the presence of light by a complex process called photosynthesis.

Animals feed by eating plants and/or other animals. The kinds of living thing they eat are limited, so it is possible to identify particular feeding relationships. For example, a fox will often get its food by killing a rabbit, the rabbit eats grass and the grass makes its own food. Such a sequence of feeding relationships is called a food chain. Similar sequences can be identified for other combinations of organisms. In all cases the food chain starts with plants of some kind.

If food is scarce, animals have to compete for what is available, and some of them will survive while others die.

3.2

Finding out children's ideas

STARTER ACTIVITIES

1 Animal and plant foods

Start by asking:

Q *What do you think animals and plants need to live?*

This should ensure that children recognize that food is needed for life. Follow this by asking more specific questions about:

- animals:

Q *Can you give me some examples of what different animals eat?*
How do you think this animal gets its food?
Do you think this animal eats anything else? Why might this be?

- plants:

Q *Where do you think plants get their food from?*
How do you think this happens?
Are there any other ways in which plants can get food?

2 Food chains

Try to establish children's ideas about food chains by asking:

Q *What do you think this animal (e.g. fox, lion) eats?*

Make sure that the animal you choose is familiar to the children and that it is carnivorous (meat-eating).

Then ask:

Q *What food do you think is eaten by the animal that the fox/lion (etc.) eats?*

Continue with this line of questioning until the children cannot go back any further.

Also ask:

Q *Is a fox/lion (etc.) eaten by anything?*

pb

V

A useful way of responding to such questions is by making a sequence of annotated drawings. There are examples of food chains in *Hábitats*.

If children use words such as 'carnivore', 'herbivore', 'predator' or 'prey', ask for clarification of what each means to them:

Q *Where have you heard the word before?*
What do you mean by that?

If they do not use such words, you might say:

Q *Some people say that a fox/lion/rabbit (etc.) is a predator/carnivore/prey animal/herbivore. What do you think they mean by that?*
Can you think of other examples?

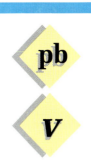

Animal
Animal's food
Food for animal's food

3 How animals and plants affect each other

Children may tend to express ideas about how animals and plants interact in response to some of the questions above and those given in 'Habitats and environmental change' (page 28). Finding out directly is not easy, but try asking:

Q

Can you make a drawing of animals and plants living together in the same place?
In what ways do you think they help each other?
In what ways do you think they do not help each other?
Do these animals and plants have to live together, or can they live apart?

Ask for clarification of the responses, as far as this is possible.

Children's ideas

Nearly all children recognize that all living things need food and can give examples. Many, however, suggest that plants get their food from the soil through their roots (see 'Children's ideas' in 'Habitats and environmental change', pages 35-6).

Food chains

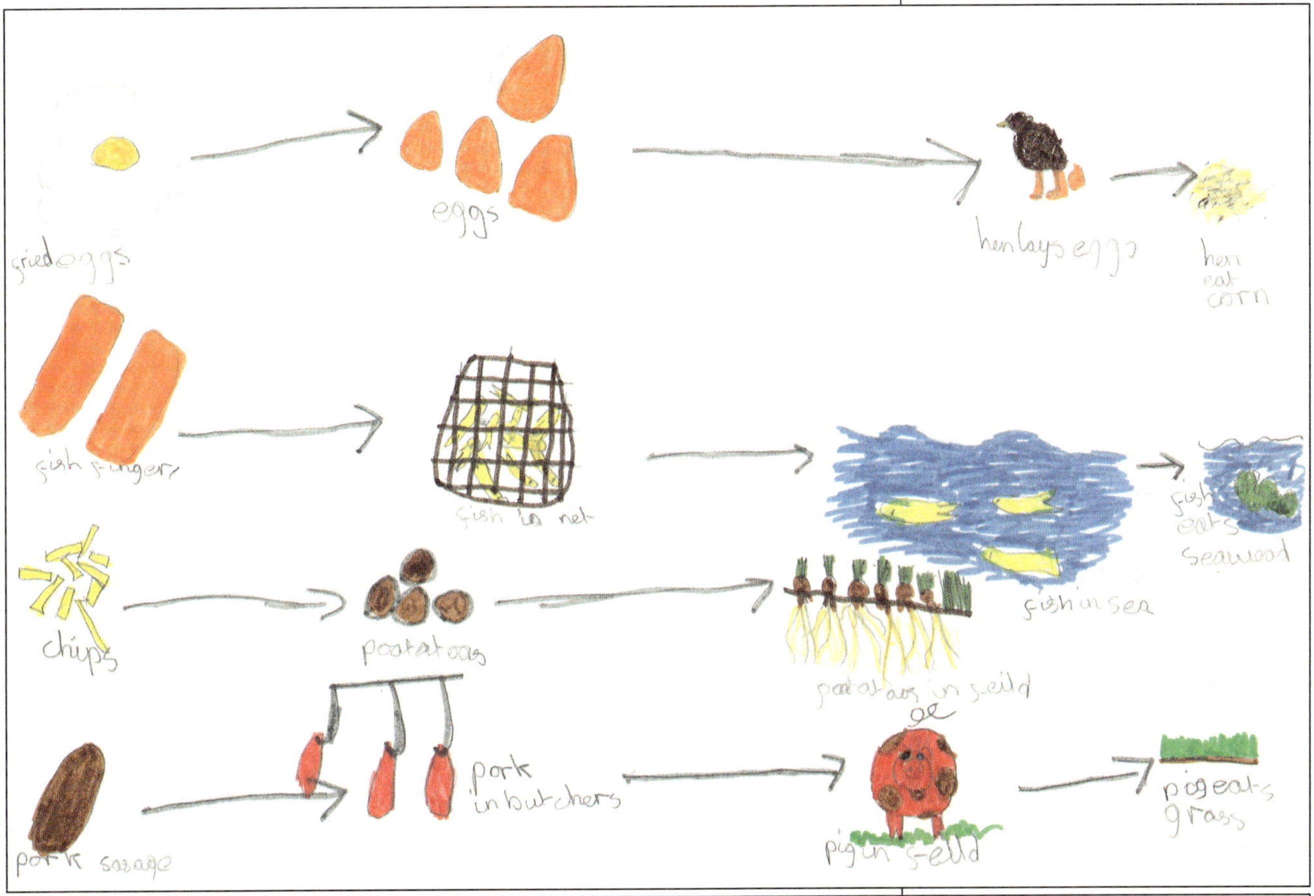

Many children consider food chains to be related to their own food, in terms of the processing which takes place. The drawing above clearly shows the idea.

Some children can relate the origin of food back to a plant and, in some cases, the Sun, as in this simple example.

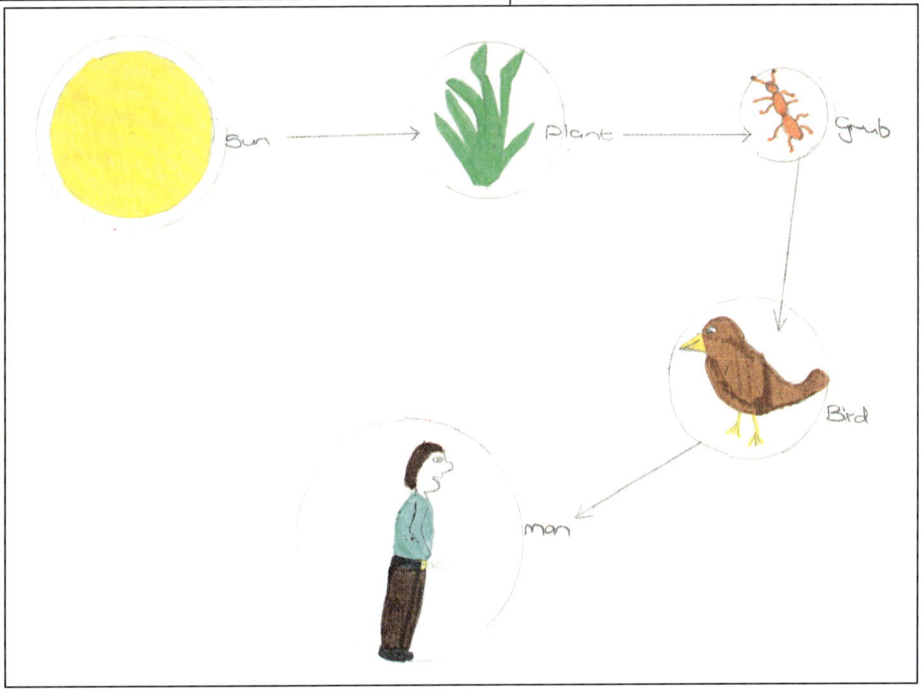

However, there are many examples of children confusing the ideas of a food chain with that of a life cycle.

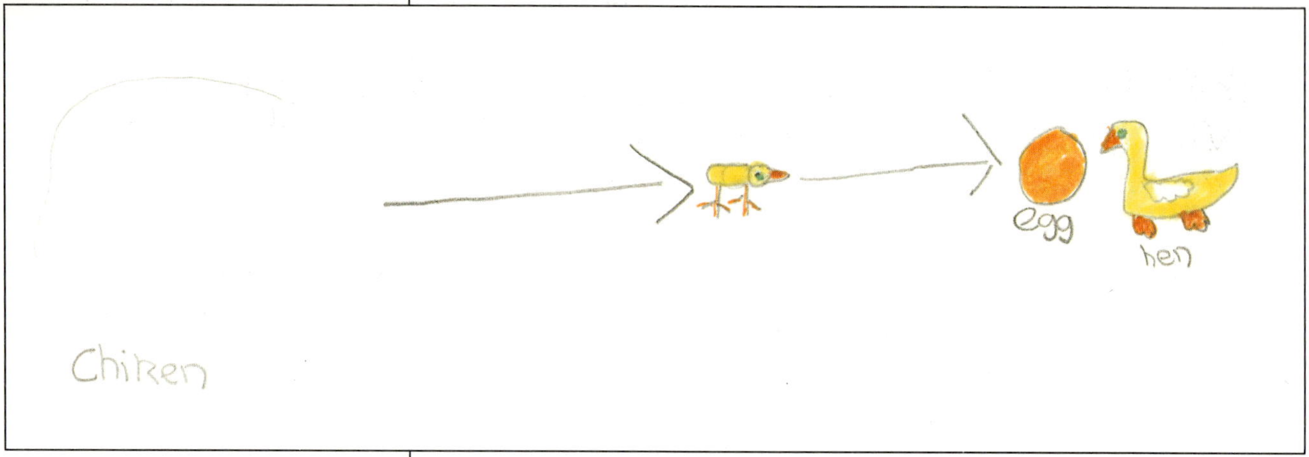

How animals and plants affect each other

Children often indicate that animals and plants do affect each other. In this example the idea of 'other animals for company' implies that there is harmony in nature.

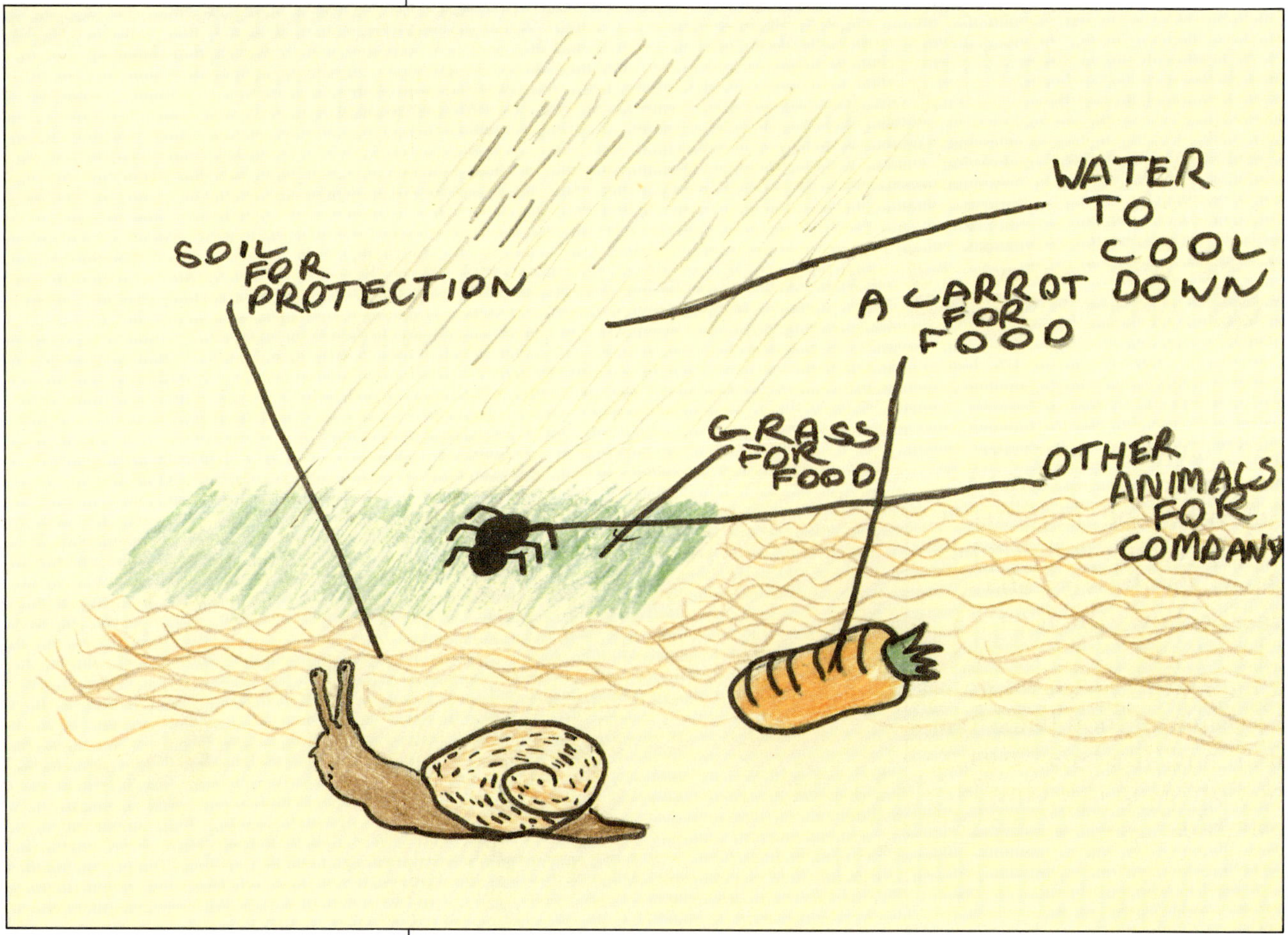

More specific references are sometimes made, as this piece of writing shows.

> The tree has got ivy all over it the ivy has killed the tree so it has no leaves on.

When questioned, the child who wrote this next piece indicated an awareness of the predator–prey relationship between spiders and flies.

> Our patch is slightly higher than the surrounding ground. There are quite a few holes going under it. There are some spider's webs, so there must be some spiders living there, and also some flies.

Helping children to develop their ideas

The chart opposite shows how you can help children to develop their ideas from starting points which have given rise to different ideas.

The centre rectangles contain starter questions.

The surrounding 'thought bubbles' contain the sorts of ideas expressed by children.

The further ring of rectangles contains questions posed by teachers in response to the ideas expressed by the children. These questions are meant to prompt children to think about their ideas.

The outer ovals indicate ways in which the children might respond to the teacher's questions.

Some of the shapes have been left blank, as a sign that other ideas may be encountered and other ways of helping children to develop their ideas may be tried.

t — PLANTS MAKE FOOD FROM CARBON DIOXIDE AND WATER, USING ENERGY FROM LIGHT. PLANTS ALSO TAKE IN NUTRIENTS FROM THE SOIL

Discussions about how plants and animals get their food are important in the development of ideas. Children may have to be introduced to the idea that plants do not get their food from the soil in the same way as animals eat food, but it is difficult to follow this up in any way other than through discussion. On the other hand, how animals get their food can be investigated in several ways.

1 What do animals eat?

AT 1 — OBSERVING

First-hand observation outside is not easy, but if opportunities arise ask children:

Q *What is the animal eating?*
How is it holding its food?
What is it using to eat its food?
Where do you think the animal gets its food from?

Encourage children to watch their pets eating. An annotated drawing could be used to show how the animal eats.

Children could make a collage of pictures collected from secondary sources, showing different animals with the food they eat. Discuss the kinds of things that are shown in the pictures, and ask:

Q *Which animals eat the same sort of food? Can you put the animals into groups?*
Which animals eat plants?

3.2

Helping children to develop their ideas about feeding relationships between organisms

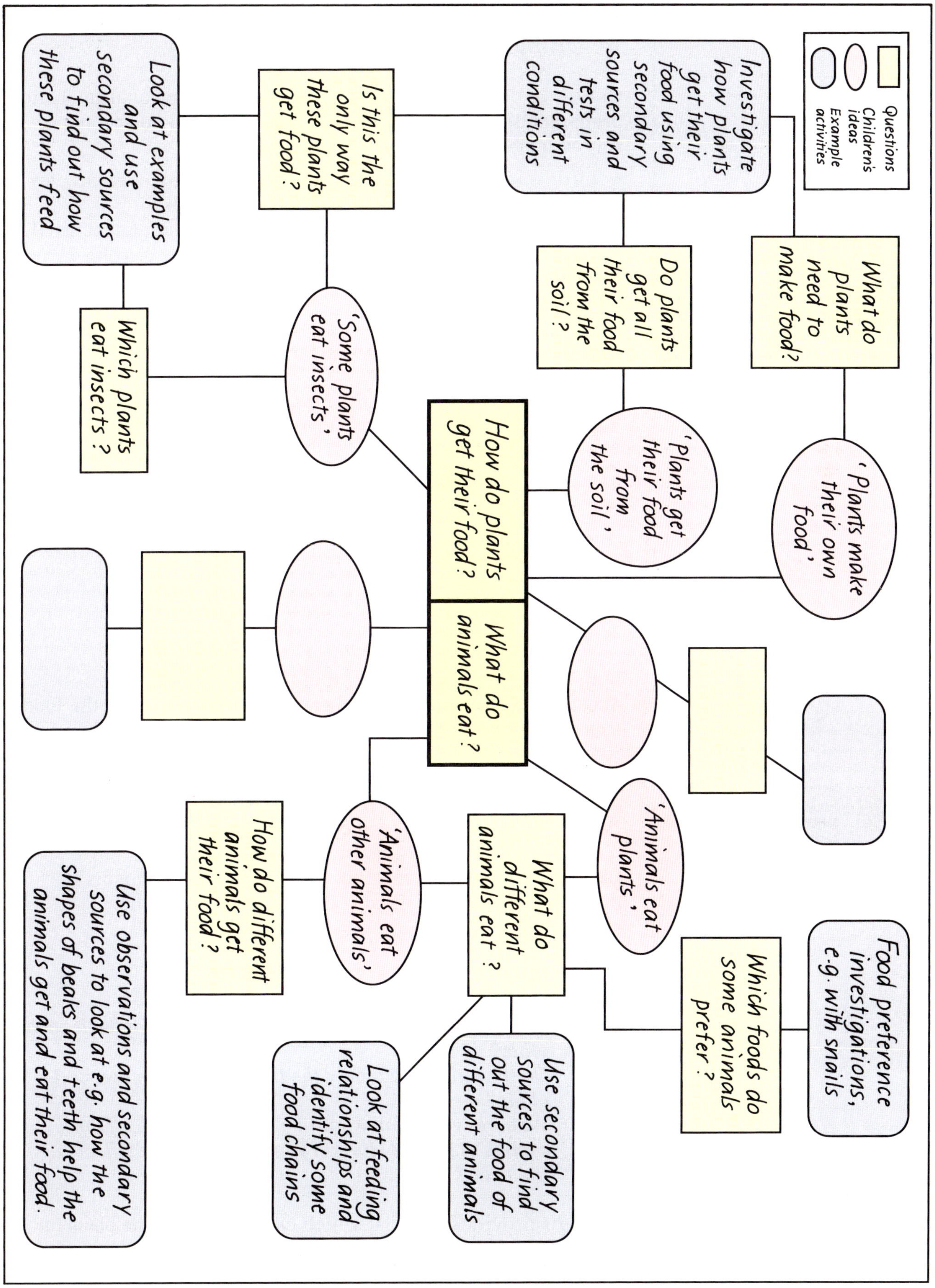

Questions
Children's ideas
Example activities
How do plants get their food?
What do animals eat?
'Plants make their own food'
What do plants need to make food?
Investigate how plants get their food using secondary sources and tests in different conditions
'Plants get their food from the soil'
Do plants get all their food from the soil?
'Some plants eat insects'
Which plants eat insects?
Is this the only way these plants get food?
Look at examples and use secondary sources to find out how these plants feed
'Animals eat plants'
What do different animals eat?
Which foods do some animals prefer?
Food preference investigations, e.g. with snails
Use secondary sources to find out the food of different animals
Look at feeding relationships and identify some food chains
'Animals eat other animals'
How do different animals get their food?
Use observations and secondary sources to look at e.g. how the shapes of beaks and teeth help the animals get and eat their food.

Which animals might be eaten by other animals?
Are there any animals which eat both plants and animals?

2 Animals' adaptations for eating

AT 1 OBSERVING

Groups of children could select a particular type of animal and prepare a display using first-hand observation and secondary source materials. Examples might include:

- birds – look for birds with different beaks and compare, for example, birds of prey with seed-eating birds;
- cats – look at the teeth and jawbones of different species of cat;
- 'minibeasts' – compare the obvious mouth parts of beetles with those of other insects.

Questions to focus these investigations could include:

Q *Do all animals of this sort feed in the same way?*
Are the beaks/teeth/jaws/mouth parts of these animals the same?
What kind of food do you think each animal of this sort eats? Can you find out?
Do you think the animal is suited to the kind of food it eats? In what ways? How do you think these help it?

3 Food chains

Both the previous activities provide starting points for developing ideas on food chains. Get children to trace the food source of a number of different animals back as far as they can. Ask:

t ALL LIVING THINGS GET THEIR FOOD ULTIMATELY FROM PLANTS

Q *Does anything eat the animal you started with?*
Where does the food come from to begin with?

Children could string together pictures of the organisms in their food chains and display them as mobiles in the classroom.

Discussion of the different food chains is needed:

Q *Do the food chains have anything in common with each other?*
Do the animals eat only the things shown in the food chain?
What do you think would happen if all of (e.g.) the rabbits died out? How do you think it would affect (e.g.) the foxes?

pb

Habitats provides material which can be used as the basis for discussion about food chains and what animals eat.

4 How animals and plants affect each other

Living things can affect each other in different ways, of which feeding is only one. Children could use secondary source materials to find out ways in which animals and plants interact.

Groups of children could discuss how particular pairs or groups of organisms affect each other, for example sea anemones and hermit crabs, flies on animals, bees and flowers, cattle egrets and cattle.

More about habitats gives examples of organisms which live together in different ways. Children could discuss how these animals benefit from each other.

pb

3.3

Waste and decay

AREAS FOR INVESTIGATION

- What happens to dead plant and animal matter?
- What is waste?
- What kinds of things are found in domestic and non-domestic waste?
- What happens to waste, including waste water?
- What effects do waste products have on the environment?

KEY IDEAS

- The remains of living things will, under suitable conditions, decay; the substances released by this can be taken in and used as nutrients by other organisms.
- Some materials change and decay quickly, while for others the changes occur over a long time.
- Materials can be re-used, recycled or discarded.
- *Many human activities produce waste materials which cause changes in the environment, locally and/or globally.

(*Asterisks indicate ideas which will be developed more fully in later key stages.)

A LOOK AT waste and decay

When something – such as a dead animal or leaves in a compost heap decays a number of things happen. The material is broken up by animals, including insects and worms; rain softens it. Bacteria and fungi feed on the remains and release nutrients back into the soil or water.

If bacteria or fungi cannot operate in the prevailing conditions, the material will not decay completely. Moisture, warmth and oxygen speed up the process of decay because these things are needed by the bacteria and fungi (though there are also anaerobic bacteria, which live without oxygen).

Some waste materials produced by human activity, such as food remnants and paper, will decay if left long enough in the right conditions. This is called biodegradable waste. Much waste, such as metal, glass and most plastics, is non-biodegradable and so is burnt or buried in large landfill sites.

Not all waste materials need to be thrown away. Many used containers, such as milk bottles, can be re-used. Other things made of glass, as well as steel and aluminium cans, plastic packaging and paper, can be recycled. Materials suitable for recycling account for approximately 40 per cent of the rubbish thrown out by the average family in Britain.

Not all forms of recycling are profitable or worthwhile. There is often a fine balance between the costs of recycling materials (collecting, sorting, and treating) and the price of raw materials. People's attitudes are a major factor in how much material is recycled.

3.3

Finding out children's ideas

STARTER ACTIVITIES

1 Decay of animals and plants

To find out how children see the process of death and decay in the environment, ask:

Q *What do you think happens to dead animals/plants?*

To help clarify the ideas children hold, you could try the following two activities.

! CARE IN HANDLING DECAYING MATTER. WASH HANDS AFTER USE. COVER CUTS AND ABRASIONS WITH PLASTERS

Place a piece of bread in a sealed transparent container and allow children to observe it over a period of time. Let the children record in a class log book what they think is happening to the bread and give suggestions about why it is happening. Dispose of the mouldy bread still in its unopened container.

e

Show children items such as leaves, grass, or animal remains and ask:

Q *If this (e.g.) leaf was left lying on the ground, what do you think might happen to it?*

If the child does not convey the idea of decay then suggest:

Q *Some people say that this (e.g.) leaf would rot. What do you think?*
What things do you know of that rot?
What do you think happens to something when it rots?
Is there anything left after something has rotted?

2 Waste products

There are a number of possible starting points here, each emphasizing a different aspect of what happens to waste products.

a Rubbish in the environment

Take the children on a walk around the immediate vicinity of the school. Ask them to identify and record the items they see that they consider to be waste or rubbish. They could do this either by listing them or by drawing them.

CARE WHEN HANDLING RUBBISH. WEAR DISPOSABLE GLOVES (OR PLASTIC BAGS) FOR LITTER SURVEYS

Ask questions such as:

Q *What makes you say that this is rubbish?*
How do you think it got there?
Where do you think it came from originally?

This work can be followed up more specifically by getting together a collection of possible waste products either from the walk or elsewhere. Try to ensure a range of items, for example:

e

- wood;
- any metal;
- plastic bag;
- hard plastic object;
- paper;
- cardboard;
- glass;
- foodstuffs (such as apple core, orange peel).

RUBBISH MAY BE CONTAMINATED: IT SHOULD BE ENCLOSED SO THAT IT CANNOT BE HANDLED. PROTECT CHILDREN FROM SHARP PIECES OF METAL OR BROKEN GLASS

Some of these, such as wood with fungus on it or mouldy apple cores, will need to be placed in sealed containers if brought into the classroom. The production of carbon dioxide during fermentation may cause the pressure inside the containers to rise: they should either be capable of withstanding the pressure or able to release the gas without releasing mould spores.

SOME PEOPLE ARE ALLERGIC TO MOULD SPORES. FERMENTATION MAY CAUSE GAS PRESSURE TO RISE

Ask questions such as:

Q *What do you think will happen to this if it is thrown away and left? What do you think makes that happen?*

v

If words such as ‘rot’, ‘disintegrate’, or ‘decay’ are used by the children, try to clarify the meaning by asking:

Q *What do you mean by that?*

Children could respond to these questions by making a sequence of annotated drawings.

b Waste produced in the home

Ask the children to make a record of all the waste products produced in their home in one day.

Encourage the children to include all the things that they consider to be waste, but avoid giving clues at this stage. An annotated list would be an appropriate record, and it could be discussed with the child by asking questions such as:

Q *Why do you think these are waste?*
Is there anything else that you think is waste in your house?

3 What happens to waste materials?

Ask the children to make a series of annotated drawings or flow charts to show what they think happens to the waste materials from their house. Ask:

Q *What happens to the rubbish you get rid of at home?*

V

Encourage the children to go as far as they can with their responses. If they use words such as 'recycle', 're-use', 'bury', or 'dump', ask for clarification:

Q *What do you mean by that?*

If the word 'recycle' is not used ask:

Q *I've heard people say that some rubbish is recycled.*
What do you think they mean by that?
Can you give me any examples of things that are recycled?
Why do you think we bother to recycle things?
Are there any things that you think could be recycled, but are not?
What would you like to recycle if it was possible? Why?

b Waste water

The above activities could also be carried out in order to gain an insight into children's ideas about what happens to waste water. Ask children to draw a series of pictures to show their ideas in response to:

Q *What happens to the water after it has gone down the plughole?*

Other questions could include:

Q *Do you think we can use water after it has been used once?*
What do you think could be done so that we can use it again?
What do you think makes the water dirty?

c Waste from non-domestic sources

To find what children recognize as waste products produced from sources other than their own home ask:

Q *Can you draw pictures of places which give out waste?*
What kinds of waste do these places make?
What do you think happens to the waste from these places?
How would you get these places to make less waste?

This activity could profitably be used alongside those on pollution given in 'Effects of human activity on the environment' (page 92).

Children's ideas

What happens to dead organisms?

Children recognize that organisms die, but their ideas about what happens after that vary. Some children think things just disappear, but others indicate that an agent, such as the wind or people or animals, has taken the dead thing away.

Teacher	*What happens to the leaf if it is just left on the ground?*
Child	*It is blown away. A caterpillar might eat it. Other things might eat it.*

Other children refer to the process of 'rotting' or 'decay' but when asked what causes this to happen they indicate conditions such as 'wet' (or 'the rain'), 'cold', 'warm'.

Teacher	*What makes it rot?*
Child	*The Sun and the rain might do that – the hotness of the Sun and the wetness of the rain.*

Very few children appear to recognize the role of micro-organisms, although some refer to other animals or creatures eating the dead thing.

Rubbish that is left on the ground

Although some children suggest that items such as paper, bread, plastic, and tin cans do not change if they are left lying on the ground, most children do indicate that something happens to them. The range of suggestions includes:

- The item just stays there.

Foil — will Just stay AND shiN

Cloth — it will get wet Damp then shrink

glass it will sTay there

- It gets dirty.

polythene = it woud be birty

- It is removed and/or eaten by animals.

◆ People might do something with it.

metal.

IF metal Was in public and Some One came Walking along the path and Started Kicking the metal. it would Full on the roud and it Would get Krushed by a car.

◆ The weather breaks it down in some way.

CarD BoarD BoX Would blowe away
yogert carton. Would bLove away.
Crisp Bag. Would blowe away
paper Warpper. Would blove away

Some children of all ages indicate that different things are affected in different ways, as shown in the next example.

Plastic – If you left Plastic in the Sun it would melt + go Small.

Tin Cans – If you left tincans in the rain it would go rusty + bend.

Polythene – If you left polythene in the Sun it would melt + go Small.

Wood – If you left wood in the rain it wood go black + moledy.

Pencil Sharpening – If you left Pencil Sharpening in the in the wind it would break up + blow away.

Card board – If you left Card board in the rain it would Sogy + Stay the Same.

References to items 'rotting' were made more frequently by older children, but their ideas about how 'rotting' took place and what caused it were varied. For example:

> *Apples rot but cans don't. Fruit comes off trees and trees have life. A can hasn't. Most things that have life can rot. Things that haven't got life don't rot.*

Very few referred to the involvement of micro-organisms such as bacteria and fungi, or mentioned that things might be biodegradable.

Rubbish from the home

Nearly all children acknowledge the role of the refuse collection services and the 'bin lorry', but when asked what happens to the rubbish afterwards they give various replies.

Some children think it is just dumped.

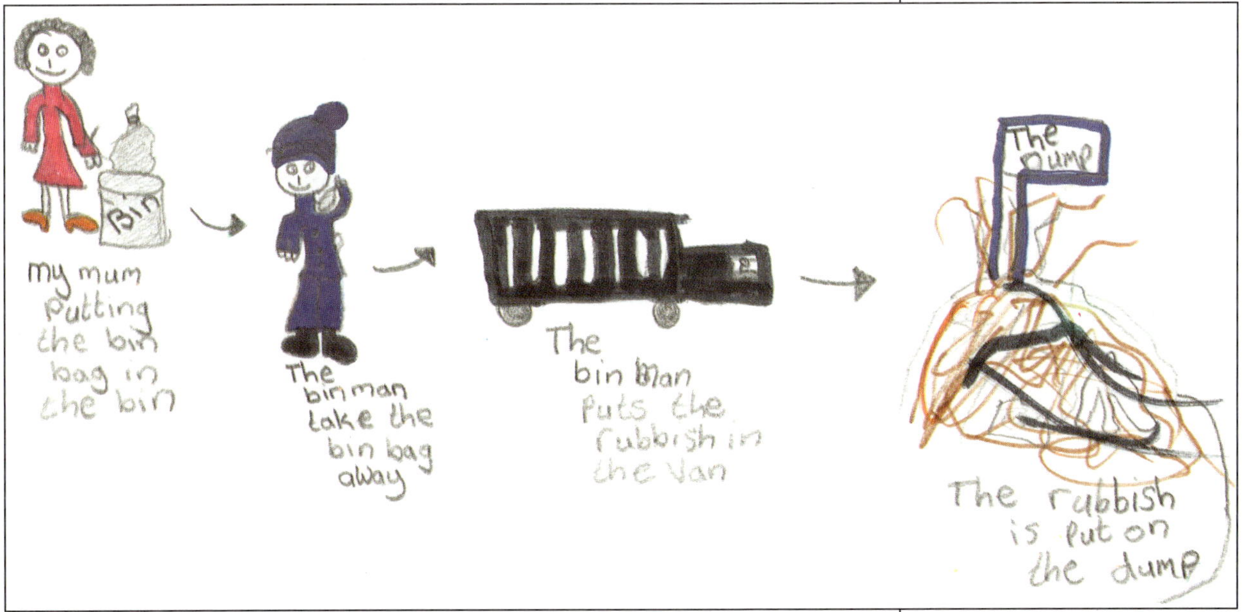

Others believe that it is dumped and burnt.

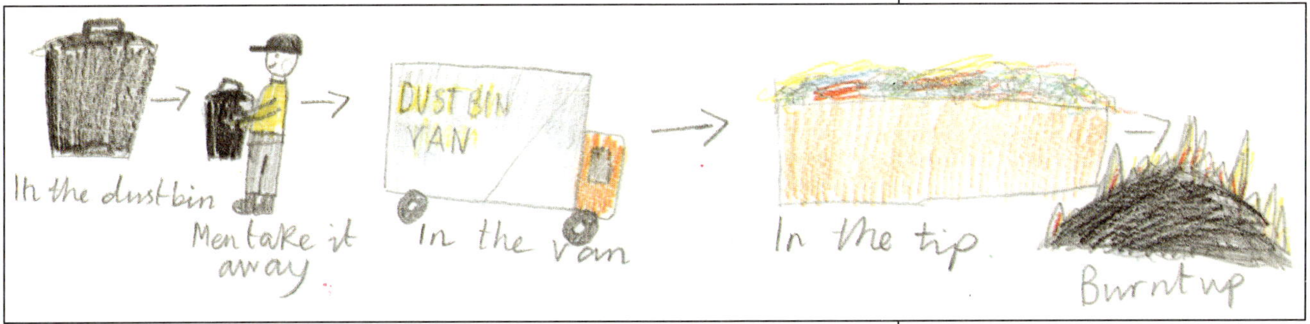

Sometimes recycling is mentioned.

Some children recognize the need to sort rubbish before treatment.

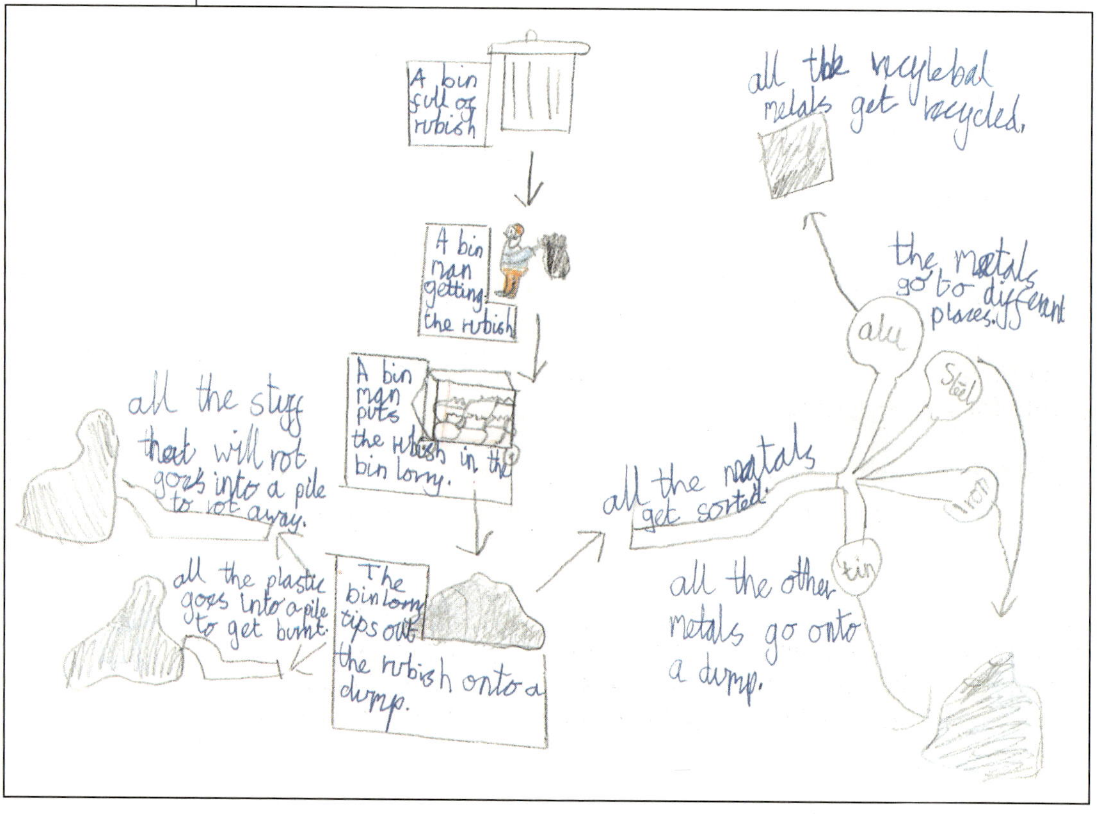

Helping children to develop their ideas

The chart overleaf shows how you can help children to develop their ideas from starting points which have given rise to different ideas.

The centre rectangles contain starter questions.

The surrounding 'thought bubbles' contain the sorts of ideas expressed by children.

The further ring of rectangles contains questions posed by teachers in response to the ideas expressed by the children. These questions are meant to prompt children to think about their ideas.

The outer ovals indicate ways in which the children might respond to the teacher's questions.

Some of the shapes have been left blank, as a sign that other ideas may be encountered and other ways of helping children to develop their ideas may be tried.

1 Conditions affecting the decay of materials

!

Safety and hygiene are essential here.
Encourage the children to identify as many examples of decaying material as they can.

Ask:

Q *In what kinds of places do you find decaying/rotting materials?*
What are the conditions like?
What do you think are the things which affect the decay of materials?

pb

Children can find further ideas in *Materials*, which looks at preservation and decay.

Use the children's responses to these questions as starting points for investigations.

e

Ask the children to design fair tests to investigate factors in the decay of materials such as bread, fruit, cardboard egg cartons or leaves.

AT 1 GENERAL

Each item should be placed in a transparent sealed container at the beginning of the test, and the whole thing disposed of unopened at the end. Suitable sealed containers are plastic bags and old lemonade bottles. Seal them sufficiently tightly to

3.3 Helping children to develop their ideas about waste and decay

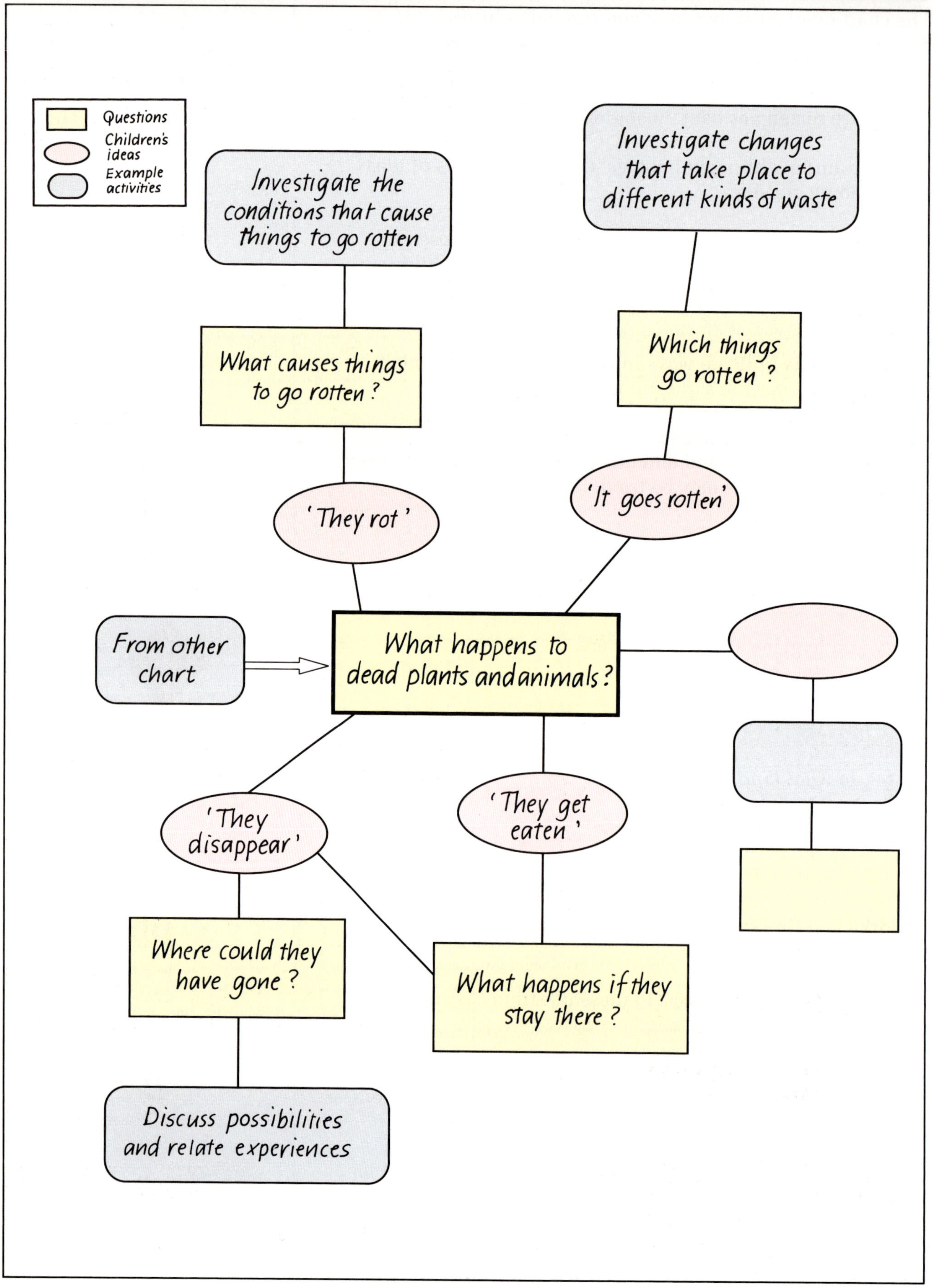
Questions
Children's ideas
Example activities
Investigate the conditions that cause things to go rotten
Investigate changes that take place to different kinds of waste
What causes things to go rotten?
Which things go rotten?
'They rot'
'It goes rotten'
From other chart
What happens to dead plants and animals?
'They disappear'
'They get eaten'
Where could they have gone?
What happens if they stay there?
Discuss possibilities and relate experiences

3.3

Helping children to develop their ideas about waste and decay (continued)

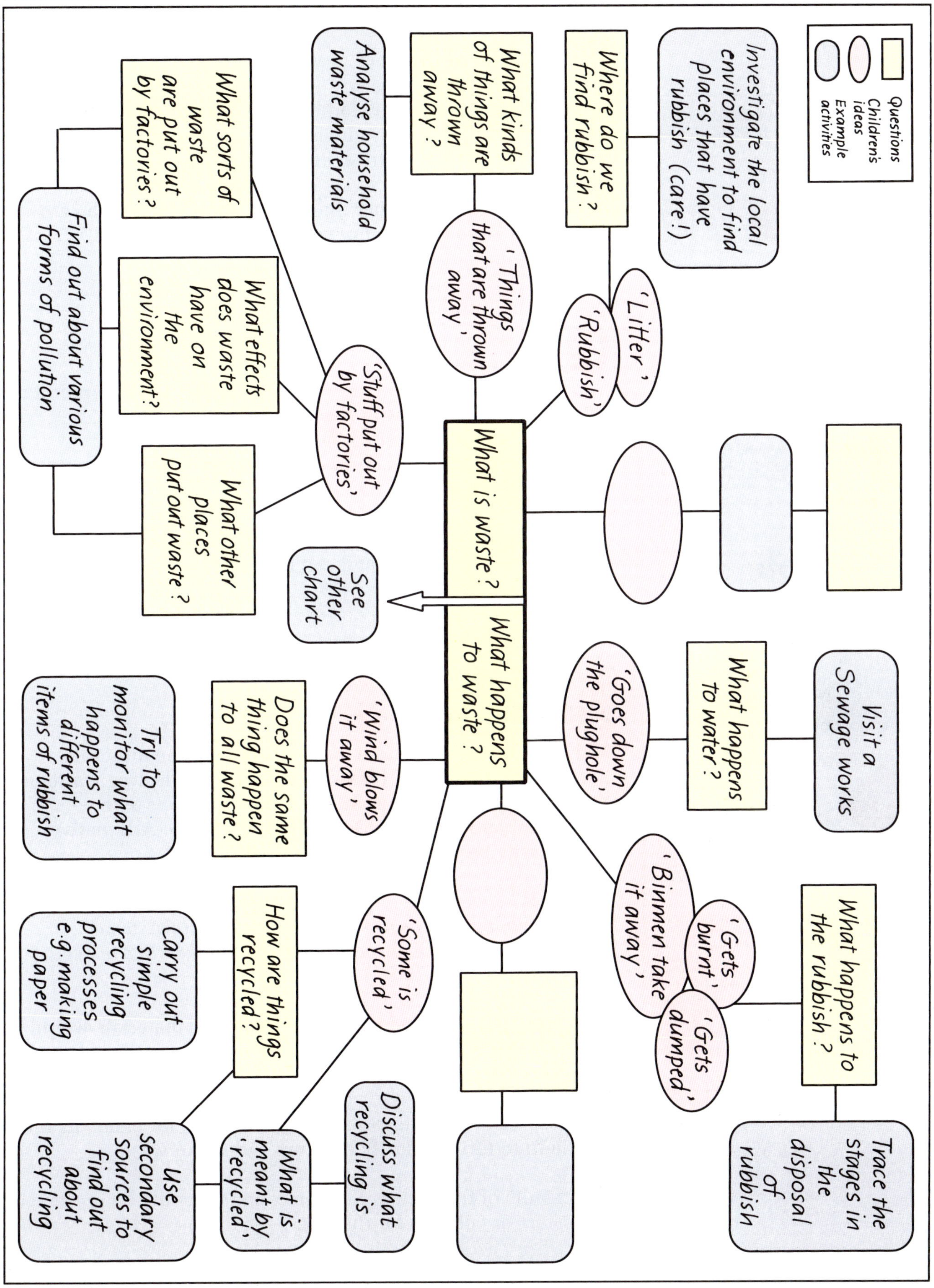
Questions
Children's ideas
Example activities
What is waste?
What happens to waste?
See other chart
'Things that are thrown away'
What kinds of things are thrown away?
Analyse household waste materials
'Litter'
'Rubbish'
Where do we find rubbish?
Investigate the local environment to find places that have rubbish (care!)
'Stuff put out by factories'
What sorts of waste are put out by factories?
What effects does waste have on the environment?
What other places put out waste?
Find out about various forms of pollution
'Goes down the plughole'
What happens to water?
Visit a Sewage works
'Wind blows it away'
Does the same thing happen to all waste?
Try to monitor what happens to different items of rubbish
'Binmen take it away'
'Gets burnt'
'Gets dumped'
What happens to the rubbish?
Trace the stages in the disposal of rubbish
'Some is recycled'
How are things recycled?
Carry out simple recycling processes e.g. making paper
What is meant by 'recycled'
Discuss what recycling is
Use secondary sources to find out about recycling

t WARMTH, MOISTURE AND AIR INCREASE RATE OF DECAY

!

t BACTERIA AND FUNGI ARE ESSENTIAL FOR DECAY OF DEAD MATTER

pb

! HYGIENE

AT 1 OBSERVING

trap spores, but not so tightly that gas from fermentation cannot escape.

Materials of the same type could be put into different conditions. For example:

- some could be in a cold, dry environment and others in a cold, damp one;
- materials could be divided between a warm and dry and a warm and damp environment;
- bread could be used fresh and toasted.

Avoid temperatures higher than about 20 °C, in case the growth of bacteria which favour human body temperature (37 °C) is encouraged.

Discuss the findings:

Q *In which conditions do things decay/rot the most quickly?*
Where might you put something if you did not want it to decay? Why would that be a good place?
What do you think might be causing the decay?
Do all materials decay in the same way/at the same speed?

More about habitats looks at examples of things which are mouldy or rotting away, and can be used to provide the basis of discussions.

2 Waste products

a Classification

Make a collection of waste materials taken from either the home or the local area. (Wear gloves when collecting waste or litter.) Ask children to group the items into their own categories, and to give reasons for their choice. Alternative criteria may be suggested, for example:

Q *Where did the item come from?*
What was it used for before it was thrown away?
How has it changed from what it looked like to begin with?

Consideration of the actual properties of the materials would link well with work on the types and uses of materials (see the *Materials* teachers' guide).

Discussions of the categories and the reasons for choosing them will help to further clarify children's ideas on waste.

The results of these classification exercises could be presented as posters or collages for display.

Many words are associated with waste, and it is worth

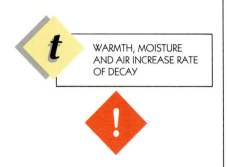

spending time on a group discussion on what is understood by some of them. They include: waste, rubbish, litter, dirt, manure, muck, rot, rust, decay, disintegrate, biodegradable, pollution, mould, recycle, re-use, discard.

V

b Litter/rubbish/waste surveys

Various surveys can be carried out to explore such questions as:

AT 1 MEASURING COMMUNICATING

Q *In which places around the school grounds does litter collect?*
How much rubbish is thrown away each day at home/in school (etc.)?
What is the most common item of rubbish that is thrown away at home/in school? (Gloves must be worn if litter is handled.)

Some attempt should be made to quantify the amounts of waste found. Ask children to suggest ways in which this could be done: for example, the number of items and the weight of material are possibilities.

! CARE WHEN HANDLING RUBBISH

Maps, charts, collages, photographs, and databases are all appropriate ways of recording the outcomes of such surveys.

it

3 What happens to waste products?

a Things that are thrown away

These include litter, garden rubbish, and old household items. Let children think of investigations to find out what happens to some of these items if they are left lying around in different places. In particular, ask:

Q *Which items do you think will stay the same and which will change?*

!

AT 1 GENERAL

t DECAY OF VEGETABLE MATTER AND FOOD INVOLVES BACTERIA AND FUNGI

AT 1 COMMUNICATING

pb

e

t FILTERING ONLY REMOVES SOLIDS; FURTHER TREATMENT IS NEEDED TO REMOVE MICRO-ORGANISMS AND CHEMICALS BEFORE WATER WOULD BE DRINKABLE

Items brought into the classroom should be placed in transparent sealed containers at the beginning of the test, and the whole thing disposed of unopened at the end. Suitable containers are plastic bags and old lemonade bottles. Anything liable to go mouldy should be sealed in sufficiently tightly to trap spores, but not so tightly that gas from fermentation cannot escape.

More specific investigations can be carried out into:

- the conditions which cause the decay of vegetable matter and waste food;
- the conditions which cause rusting and changes in other metals.

See also 'Types and uses of materials' in the *Materials* teachers' guide.

Other investigations might follow questions such as:

Q *What happens if something is buried?*
Which things change if they are left in water?
Is it possible to stop things rotting?

b Things that are taken away in the bin lorry

This may be studied by using secondary sources, but ideally it should be linked with a visit and/or talks by the local refuse collectors. Children could follow this up as 'newspaper reporters' writing a piece for the local paper or school magazine.

Habitats has information about 'rubbish tips' and can be used for further discussion.

c Things that go down the plughole

Trace what happens to water and other things that get washed down the drain. Use secondary sources, combined if possible with visits to sewage works and waterworks. Children could be given some water containing particles of earth and asked:

Q *Can you find a way to clean this water?*

A simple filter could be used.

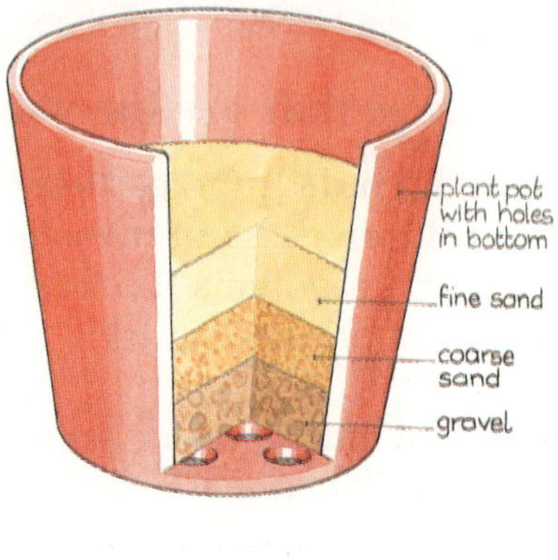

A discussion of the processes should help distinguish between the removal of solid materials (soil, cans, etc.), organisms (both harmful and harmless) and chemical substances (lead, washing powder, etc.).

This activity would fit into work on water pollution (see 'Effects of human activity on the environment', page 106).

Habitats encourages children to think about what happens to water (and everything else) which goes down the drain.

pb

4 What can be recycled?

Ask children to suggest which kinds of waste can be recycled or re-used. Make a collection of rubbish and get children to sort out the items that can be recycled or re-used.

Concentrate on these and separate them into similar materials, for example glass, paper, metal and plastic. Ask:

Q

Why do you think we need to sort materials?
How do you think you could help in this process?
How much do you think it costs to recycle materials?

Children could also discover where there are bottle banks and newspaper collection points in the area.

Use secondary sources to help children investigate what happens when things are:

- recycled – bottles, tins, paper, plastic;
- re-used – milk bottles.

!

CHILDREN MUST WEAR GLOVES IF THEY HANDLE RUBBISH, AND ANY TABLES WILL NEED TO BE CLEANED WITH DISINFECTANT

t

RECYCLING COSTS MONEY

3.3

pb

Habitats considers things which can be recycled. Children could also look at *More about materials* for ideas about sorting and recycling waste.

Carry out a survey in school of things that have been recycled and/or re-used for any purpose. For example:

- yoghurt pots for paint pots, modelling;
- bottles for watering plants, as vases;
- old toys for other children;
- newspapers for covering desks.

Children could do some recycling themselves by:

e

- making paper;
- designing and making paper sandals, hats;
- using stale (but not mouldy) bread for making bread-and-butter pudding;
- making models out of papier-mâché;
- making toys out of old wood and metal.

Discuss:

Q *Why do you think we should recycle and re-use materials?*
What are the advantages and disadvantages of recycling?

Try to encourage children to look for examples of recycling on a large scale. Relate the work to the limitations of the Earth's resources if appropriate.

5 How can we reduce the amount of waste?

Make a collection of items that could be included in a typical weekly shopping trip. Include both food and non-food items. Encourage children to examine the type and quantity of packaging found on each item. Ask them:

Q *Which parts of the packaging do you think are really necessary?*
Do similar items (for example, packets of cakes) all have the same amount of packaging?
What are the different parts of the packaging for?
Can you suggest other ways of packaging the items?

Children could design their own packaging for certain items. Encourage children to consider ways of reducing the amount of waste and rubbish at home and at school. They might keep a log for, say, two weeks, and:

AT 1 GENERAL

- in week 1, record the amount of rubbish thrown away as usual;
- in week 2, put into action the suggested ways of reducing the amount of rubbish and record what is actually thrown away.

Compare the two weeks and discuss the value of the actions taken. Groups of children could devise their own tests to investigate the effectiveness of ways to reduce rubbish and waste. Are the tests fair?

Secondary sources could be used to help children consider ways of reducing waste on a larger scale – locally, nationally and globally.

3.4 Effects of human activity on the e

AREAS FOR INVESTIGATION

Work in this area may readily be combined with aspects of *Materials*, *Rocks, soil and weather*, and Geography. Work on 'Waste and decay' (page 72) can easily be linked to many of the investigations in this section.

Children can explore:

- different human activities that take place around them, such as farming and industry;
- local projects to improve the surroundings;
- issues of international concern, such as the 'greenhouse effect';
- the merits of and problems with particular planning proposals;
- what is meant by 'pollution'.

KEY IDEAS

- Human activity has changed all parts of the environment.
- The resources of the Earth are finite.

A LOOK AT the effects of human activities on the environment

Human activity has had an effect on the environment for thousands of years, and there is nowhere on Earth that has escaped such effects completely. It is important to recognize that not all human activity is bad for the environment. Much is being done for the conservation of landscapes and of species near to extinction.

The effects of human activities can be clearly seen in urban, rural and 'natural' areas of the environment, both locally and globally. Humans affect the environment by:

- using it to provide food through farming and fishing;
- extracting raw materials by quarrying and mining;
- depleting the limited reserves of fossil fuels;
- building roads and railways, towns and cities;
- putting into the environment large amounts of materials which affect other living things;
- conserving areas, for example nature reserves.

In recent years the adverse global effects of some human activities have been recognized. These include:

- acid rain;
- destruction of the rainforests;
- the greenhouse effect causing global warming;
- the depletion of the ozone layer.

Finding out children's ideas

STARTER ACTIVITIES

1 Our surroundings and the way people have changed them

You could take children out to look at any view from the school grounds. Use a sheet of paper divided into three sections, and ask them to draw the view in the middle section. Then ask them to consider:

Q *What do you think it would have been like if no one had ever come here?*
What do you think it would look like in the future if all the people had long since gone away?

Children could draw their ideas in on the other two sections.

What it used to look like before people came	What it is like now	What it would look like if all the people went away

Ask the children to annotate their drawings. You might also talk with them to clarify what they have represented.

2 An area without people

Ask children to imagine an area of the country that no person has ever been to.

Q *What do you think it would be like?*

They could show their ideas in a drawing.

3 Areas with people

a Use of pictures

Make (or ask the children to collect) a display of a variety of pictures showing different areas which have been affected by human activity. Include some areas where there has been little if any human influence. The pictures could include:

- a farming area;

e

- industry;
- hills and lakes;
- recreation areas;
- the sea;
- a town.

You could display the pictures together with the question:

Q *What things on each picture have been done by people?*

Leave the display for some days to allow children to consider their ideas before discussing these with them, either in small groups or as a whole class.

b Visits to areas

If you have the opportunity to visit an area such as those mentioned above, this could provide a focus for questions about human activity in that area.

! FOLLOW SCHOOL OR LEA GUIDELINES ON VISITS

Q *What sort of things have people done to make it look like that?*
How have people affected this place?

4 Local projects

Discover the children's awareness of local projects to improve the environment.

Q *Can you think of anything that people are doing to make this neighbourhood better to live in?*
What would you do to make this place better to live in?
What would make these changes difficult to carry out?
What things do people do which are not good for the place where you live?

You could ask children to discuss their ideas in small groups, and to record their responses to the questions in writing.

5 Environmental issues

a Looking at labels

e

v

Display some items with 'green' labels and words such as 'environmentally friendly' written on them.

Give children time to examine the items. Draw their attention to the words 'environment' and 'environmentally'.

Q *Have you heard these words before?*
What do you think they mean?

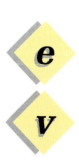

b Media reports

Children may be stimulated by environmental issues that are presented in newspapers and on television. These may be local issues, or global ones such as the depletion of the ozone layer or the greenhouse effect. Take the opportunity to ask for their ideas.

Q *What do you think this effect is?*
Why do you think it is happening?
What can we do about it?

c Pollution

Ask children to bring in newspaper reports or other items which use the word 'pollution'. Ask them to think about what the word means. They could write down their own ideas in response to:

Q *Have you heard the word 'pollution'?*
What does it mean to you?

Children's ideas

Children readily recognize human influence on the environment when they see people in the context of that influence. Buildings, for example, are invariably accepted as the result of people's activity. It is when children come to things that could have either human or natural causes that their opinions are more likely to differ. They may regard trees in the countryside, for instance, as all planted or all naturally occurring. It is less common for children to reveal an awareness of both possibilities.

> *Well, some trees might have been planted by people but those weren't.*

Some things in the countryside may look extremely 'natural' and yet have been originated by people. A hedge, despite the obvious influence of trimming, looks natural; and indeed many of the species found in hedgerows have come to be there through natural causes. The line of the hedge, however, betrays its human origins (as a boundary), no matter how long ago it was planted. Children may not recognize the human influence in a traditional rural environment, in view of the great changes brought about by more recent agricultural practices.

In contrast, younger children tend to see human influence everywhere. They may believe nothing happens without a human cause. This tendency to over-generalize human influence may be stronger in children who live in urban surroundings.

Some children think that hills were made by people; perhaps this is a result of seeing earth being moved in parks and building sites.

> *Sometimes people put them there. They put rocks there and cover them up with grass – they do – big ones and little ones.*

Children's drawing of what places could have been like before people came (or after they had gone away) may reveal both awareness of the effects people have had and opinions about it. The pictures on page 98 and 99 were drawn by children who live in an urban area.

Some children appear to focus more on the negative aspects of human influence, such as litter and vandalism, while nature is seen as attractive. Younger children, in particular, think of local and immediate problems – especially litter. Older children are more likely to show awareness of less obvious, even international, problems such as pollution by car fumes and deforestation; they often suggest specific solutions to the problems.

if No one had ever been there all the grass would be very long and there would be No flowers at all there because noone lives there
It would be eat grass and flowers growing every where and trees in the garden.
It would be all Messy and rubbish would be in the garden and weeds would got tangled round all the flowers

[People] drop litter – you're not supposed to. You should put it in the bin to make it tidier.

Bad men smash the windows and do the houses in.

People use cans which are not ozone-friendly. They should use ozone-friendly cans.

When asked about what could be done to improve the area where they live, children are as likely to talk about changes to people's behaviour, improvements to their own homes and better amenities as they are about improvement to the landscape or townscape. Improving the townscape is generally associated with planting schemes.

> *Pick up rubbish and build more houses.*
>
> *Make a fine on people who do graffiti and vandalism. Put a big fence around the pond because people just wreck the pond. Reduce the price for converting cars to unleaded petrol – every car should have a converted engine.*
>
> *Build new walls and gates and paint them. Make it look nice with flower pots. Make it look different – not everything the same.*

The words 'pollution' and 'environment' are unfamiliar to many younger children. Older children may be able to give extensive explanations.

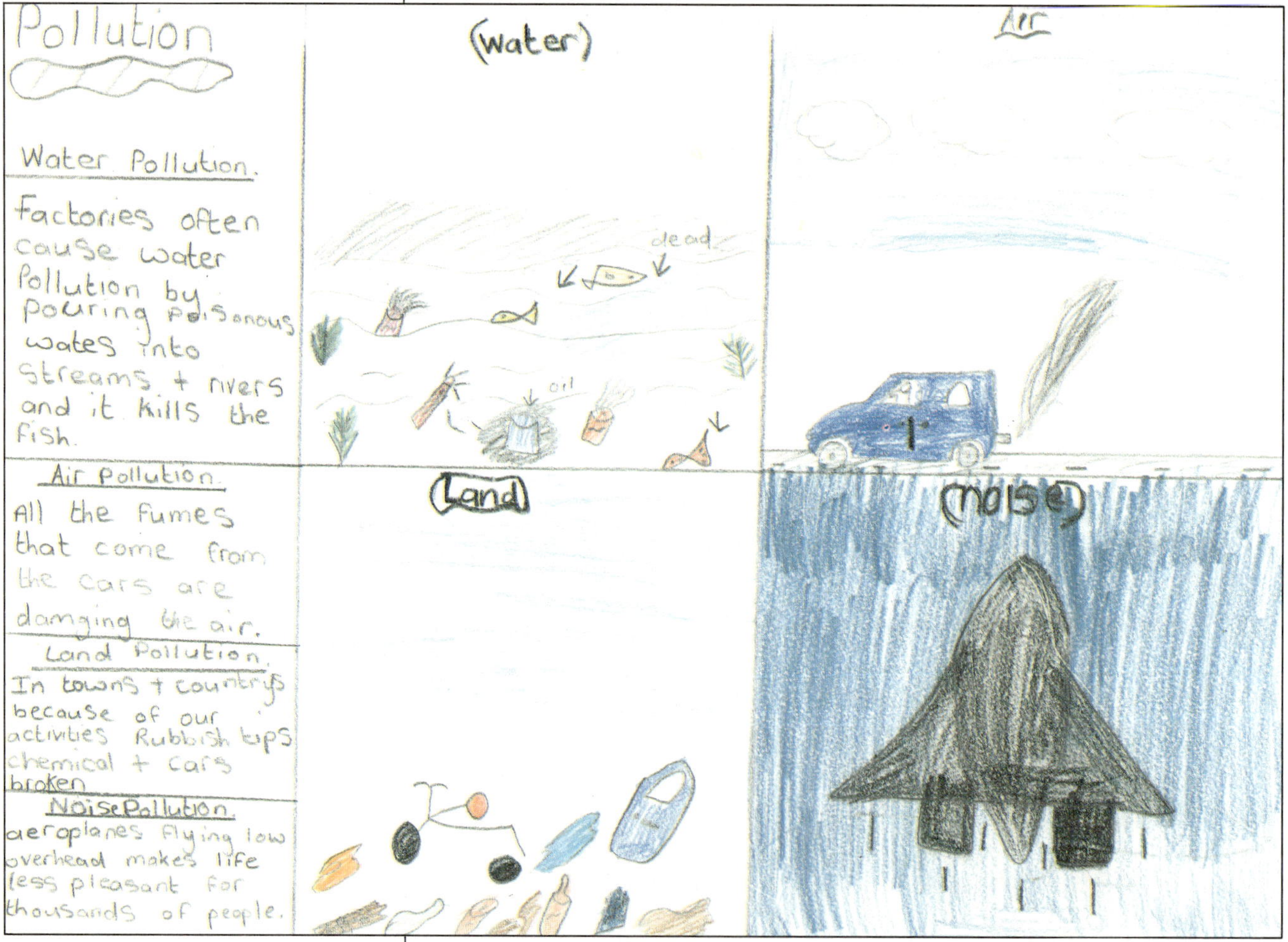

Among meanings they attribute to 'environment' are:

> - *the place where you live;*
> - *all animals and plants;*
> - *everywhere;*
> - *us and the things we are doing;*
> - *houses and people.*

Pollution is more likely to be associated with single events and disasters than with continuing or global problems. It may be particularly linked with the contamination of the sea, especially by oil. Children may be strongly influenced here by current news. Air pollution is less prevalent in children's minds, although older children may have detailed ideas about the effects of factories, car fumes and aerosol sprays.

Other harmful environmental effects such as noise are rarely mentioned.

> *Polluting the air with all the fumes casting a screen over the Earth like with 'greenhouse effect'.*

The idea of 'light pollution' in urban areas, which is mainly the effect of street lights, has also been noticed by a few children. Many children living in urban areas may never have seen the stars in a clear night sky.

3.4

Helping children to develop their ideas

The chart opposite shows how you can help children to develop their ideas from starting points which have given rise to different ideas.

The centre rectangles contain starter questions.

The surrounding 'thought bubbles' contain the sorts of ideas expressed by children.

The further ring of rectangles contains questions posed by teachers in response to the ideas expressed by the children. These questions are meant to prompt children to think about their ideas.

The outer ovals indicate ways in which the children might respond to the teacher's questions.

Some of the shapes have been left blank, as a sign that other ideas may be encountered and other ways of helping children to develop their ideas may be tried.

1 Changes in the local environment

Help children to appreciate how their locality has changed over time.

AT 1 OBSERVING

t HUMAN INFLUENCES ON THE ENVIRONMENT ARE WIDESPREAD, IN RURAL AS WELL AS URBAN AREAS

a Changes taking place today

Ask children to look at changes actually taking place. These could include:

- an area being demolished;
- a field becoming a building site;
- an area of derelict housing being demolished and being made into a park;
- pasture being converted to arable farming;
- official footpaths being marked in the countryside.

Children could draw 'before' and 'after' pictures.

b Changes from some time ago

Invite an older person who has always lived locally to come and talk to the children. Ask her or him to talk about changes in the appearance of the area. Encourage the children to think about which of these changes were caused by people and which, if any, occurred naturally. This work could be developed into a historical project, with the focus on what people have done to their surroundings. Use books, old photographs and newspapers for information. Ask children to think about what improvements have been made to the area and what deterioration has taken place. These are sometimes

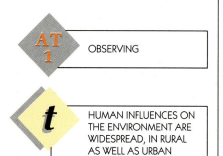

Helping children to develop their ideas about the effects of human activity on the environment

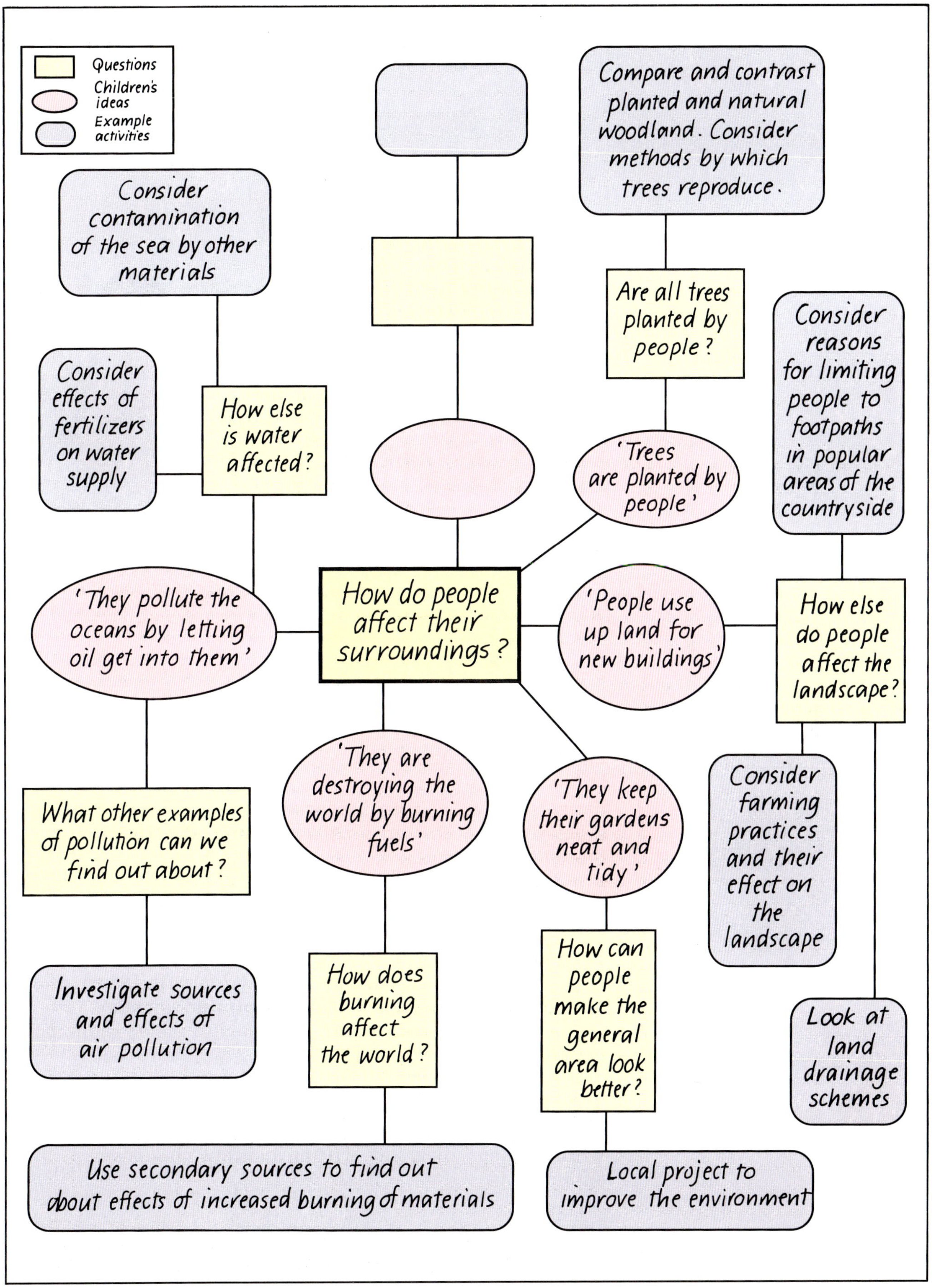

Questions
Children's ideas
Example activities
Compare and contrast planted and natural woodland. Consider methods by which trees reproduce.
Consider contamination of the sea by other materials
Are all trees planted by people?
Consider reasons for limiting people to footpaths in popular areas of the countryside
Consider effects of fertilizers on water supply
How else is water affected?
'Trees are planted by people'
'They pollute the oceans by letting oil get into them'
How do people affect their surroundings?
'People use up land for new buildings'
How else do people affect the landscape?
'They are destroying the world by burning fuels'
'They keep their gardens neat and tidy'
Consider farming practices and their effect on the landscape
What other examples of pollution can we find out about?
Investigate sources and effects of air pollution
How does burning affect the world?
How can people make the general area look better?
Look at land drainage schemes
Use secondary sources to find out about effects of increased burning of materials
Local project to improve the environment

matters of value judgement, and children should be prepared for differences of opinion. Is the new shopping complex better than the old market, for example? Are bigger fields better than small enclosures?

AT 1 COMMUNICATING

One way for children to report their findings is in the form of a class newspaper. This might include both reporting of changes and commenting on them.

c Looking at particular human activities

Children might do project work on specific activities in the local environment, such as farming, building or industry. Encourage them to find out about what is used, what actually happens and what causes waste to be produced (see 'Waste and decay', page 72). This could form a combined science and geography project. Use of materials can be considered among the scientific aspects.

pb

More about habitats can be used as the basis of a discussion about the effects that farming has on the landscape and its inhabitants. You may also find *Rocks, soil and weather* useful – it has a spread describing one particular farm in Devon. *More about habitats* gives an example of how one scientist influenced farming practices and helped in the development of new products from peanuts.

! CHECK YOUR SCHOOL'S POLICY ON VISITS

A visit might be arranged, and this would form the focus for subsequent work. Let children record their findings in a poster with drawings, diagrams, writing and flow charts, as appropriate.

Different groups of children could work on different activities.

d A local planning proposal

As a follow-up to the work on particular human activities, you could use a local planning issue to stimulate debate. There may be proposals for road building, redesignation of land use, house building or industrial sites. Local newspapers should prove useful sources, and council offices should also be ready to furnish information.

e

Ask children to think of arguments for and against a particular proposal. You might then use this, or an imaginary situation, for a role-playing exercise. Some children can argue in support of a proposal, others can be opponents. A third group of children can listen to the arguments and form a judgement on the proposal.

AT 1 COMMUNICATING

e Revisiting earlier activities

At this point, it would be appropriate to return to any of the first three activities that children have done.

If children did the activity on 'Changes taking place today' (page 102), small groups of them might look at the picture again. Let them consider whether they have noticed all the changes that might have been brought about by people. Encourage them to discuss this with one another.

If children worked on 'Changes from some time ago' and/or 'Looking at particular human activities' (pages 102 and 104) they could consider their ideas again in groups. Ask them to compare the different ideas they had about what a place would be like without people.

You may find *Rocks, soil and weather* useful – it contains photographs of landscapes and asks children how they think they have been affected by human activity.

pb

2 Environmental improvement – a local project

t PEOPLE OFTEN HAVE DIFFERENT OPINIONS ABOUT WHAT KIND OF IMPROVEMENTS THEY WANT

There may be a local project to improve the environment in some way – the construction of a nature reserve, the restoration of wasteland, the cleaning or renovation of old buildings. If possible, arrange a visit. You may be able to involve the children in the project, as well as help them to become aware of it. Someone from the project may be prepared to come and talk about it. Encourage the children to think of questions to ask.

! FOLLOW SCHOOL OR LEA GUIDELINES ON VISITS

e

AT 1 COMMUNICATING

t SOME HUMAN ACTIVITIES HAVE GLOBAL CONSEQUENCES

3 Raising awareness of environmental issues

Follow up the discussions that took place in the activity on 'Environmental issues' (page 95). You will need secondary sources for information on the issues in which children are interested. They could themselves write to various organizations. Let them present the 'issue' on a poster. Ask questions such as the following to guide children in the extraction of appropriate information from the secondary sources and its presentation in their own words:

Q *What is happening?*
What is making it happen?
Do all people agree on what is making it happen?
How can we stop this happening?

v

There will be opportunities during this work for the development of vocabulary. Children could, for example, add to the display of 'environmentally friendly' labels and items. You could ask them to write sentences with the word 'environment' in them. Other words will arise as children find out about environmental issues. Ask children to discuss the meaning they attach to a word with one another.

pb

More about habitats encourages children to think carefully about what is meant by being 'environmentally friendly' – in particular, the relative merits of paper and polystyrene cups. The children could consider a glass bottle and a plastic bottle in the same way.

4 Pollution

Extend children's awareness of pollution:

- as both a local and a global event;
- as a continuous process as well as individual disasters;
- in its various forms:

air pollution (smoke, acid rain, car and industrial fumes, damage to the ozone layer, burning of rainforests);
water pollution (sewage, fertilizers, lead pipes, oil in the sea);
litter (see 'Waste and decay', page 87);
noise (airports, roads, loud music - see *Sound and music*);
visual (eyesores, vandalism);
light spillage (preventing sight of the night sky).

pb

Set up a pollution noticeboard. Ask children to report and display instances of pollution. They could use newspaper cuttings or their own pictures and writing.

e

There are also a number of simple activities that children can do to record or to see the effects of pollution.

e

i Smear Vaseline thinly over cards and hang them in various places outside to detect 'bits' in the air. Hang the cards for the same length of time. Ask:

Q *Can you find a way of estimating the 'dirtiness' of the cards?*

More about habitats encourages children to consider some of the problems caused by pollution in the air.

pb

ii Grow cress seeds, some normal and some that have been soaked in water polluted with household chemicals (such as disinfectant, bleach, hair dye).

e

!

Bleach and disinfectants are corrosive, and children must not have access to them. High concentrations of chemicals may be needed to show effects. Teachers should use rubber gloves. Warn the children not to pollute seeds for themselves or to handle the seeds.

This may be a good opportunity to teach children the meanings of the international warning symbols.

CHAPTER 4 Assessment

4.1 Introduction

You will have been assessing your children's ideas and skills by using the activities in this teachers' guide. This on-going, formative assessment is essentially part of teaching since what you find is immediately used in suggesting the next steps to help the children's progress. But this information can also be brought together and summarized for purposes of recording and reporting progress. This summary of performance has to be in terms of National Curriculum level descriptions at the end of the key stages, and some schools keep records in terms of levels at other times.

This chapter helps you summarize the information you have from children's work in terms of level descriptions. Examples of work relating to the theme of this guide are discussed and features which indicate activity at a certain level are pointed out to show what to look for in your pupils' work as evidence of achievement at one level or another. It is necessary, however, to look across the full range of work, and not judge from any single event or piece of work.

There are two sets of examples provided. The first is the assessment of skills in the context of the activities related to the concepts covered in this guide. The second deals with the development of these concepts.

4.2 Assessment of skills (AT1)

Things to look for when pupils are investigating living things in their environment, as indicating progress from level 2 to level 5:

Level 2: Making suggestions as well as responding to others' suggestions about how to find things out or compare the conditions in which different plants and animals live. Using equipment such as magnifying glasses, tweezers and droppers, in making observations. Recording what they find and comparing it with what they expected.

Level 3: Saying what they expect to happen when something is changed and suggesting ways of collecting information to test their predictions. Carrying out fair tests, knowing why they are fair, and making measurements. Recording what they find in a variety of ways; noticing any patterns in it.

Level 4: Making predictions which guide the planning of fair tests. Using suitable equipment and making adequate and relevant observations. Using tables and charts to record measurements and other observations. Interpreting, drawing conclusions and attempting to relate findings to scientific knowledge.

Level 5: Planning controlled investigations of predictions which are based on scientific knowledge. Using equipment carefully, repeating observations as necessary. Using line graphs to record and help interpretation; considering findings in relation to scientific knowledge.

The class was considering how waste materials might change over a period of time. The teacher focused on how things in the classroom which were thrown away might change. The children were asked to make predictions about what would happen to some of these objects. They predicted that some would stay the same while others would rot or disintegrate. Seth and Steven wrote down what they thought.

Seth

Plastic The Plastic would Crinkle up.

Tin Can The Tin Can Would have rust on.

Polythene The polythene would rip and be dirty

Wood The wood would start to rot.

Pencil Sharpenings The Pencil sharpenings would blow away

plastic I think the plastic would get turned into the ground after a year or so.

Glass the glass would probabley go into the earth and some of it would go back into Sand.

wood the wood would probabley get wet and rott.

Foodstuffs the foodstuff would go mouldy and the things like cans can rust and be dangerous to things like animals

Metal Metal can rust and cut people so it would be good if it rotted but it doesn't.

Steven

Following the discussion of the children's ideas, the class was divided into groups. Some groups selected a range of materials and recorded their present appearance, and said or drew how they expected the materials might change. The materials were then put on a shelf (in safe packaging where necessary) so that the children could monitor any changes as they occurred. Pauline's drawings (overleaf) show the changes she noticed in a group of objects.

Pauline

dry Shell
it,s gone Dirty round the edge with heat
Banna dry Skin
it,s gone black And Sogy because it,s been Stuk in a case with no air For along time
cheese dry
it,s gone all molDy becouse it,s been trapped in a case For a long time
Foil dry
Foil crinkled up and Stuk to the Side becouse it get,s Stiky With heeat
apple. dry
it,s gone sogy and brown becouse it hasent been protected
Bread dry
Dirty and Stale round the edge becouse it,s got no roome or no Air

Joanne

We got some plastic bags. Then we got some bread and put it into 4 bags. We put 6 drops of water into two of the bags and left the other two dry.

We put the bag with water in on the windowsill and we put the bag with no water in on the windowsill The Other two bags we put in a cold Place in the cupboard.

Paul

Joanne, Paul and Gary were among a group who explored how different conditions might affect changes in bread. They put both wet and dry bread in both warm and cold conditions, although in Joanne's description she does not mention the test of temperature as well as of the effect of water.

Pauline's work describes her observations. She has mentioned some of the factors which she believes have influenced the changes. Pauline's work demonstrates an ability to make relevant observations, indicating level 2. The teacher could use her ideas about possible explanations for the changes as a basis for further investigations, thus helping her progress towards level 3.

we put four pieces of bread in 4 separate bags.

we put one in a cold cupbourd

we put one on the window sill

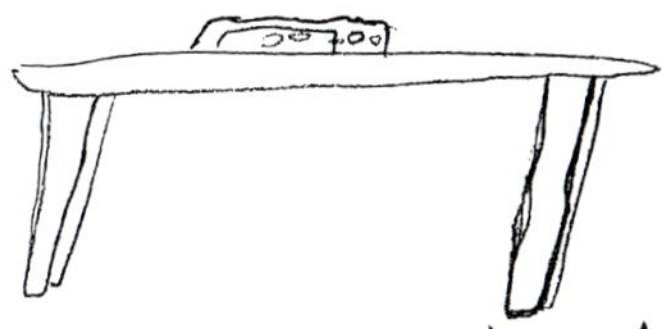

I think the cold and wet will rott first. And secondly I think the hot and wet will next.

Gary	*The bread in the warm rotted first.*
Teacher	*Why do you think that happened?*
Gary	*If it's warm it will rot.*

Gary

Seth and Steven stated how they would expect various items to change; this part of their investigation is at level 3. Steven shows rather more knowledge, but it would be necessary to find out how both of them might follow up their ideas in a investigation in order to confirm achievement at level 3.

Paul and his group investigated the effect on bread of a combination of wet, dry, warm and cold conditions. Paul's account shows a clear attempt to control the conditions in order to compare them and this indicates progress towards level 3. There is no sign in his account of controlling the amount of bread and water and it would be necessary to discuss with him whether he had considered these to be important things to keep the same before deciding the extent to which he was aware of carrying out a fair test. Joanne, on the other hand, has controlled the amount of water.

Gary's work also indicates aspects of achievement at level 3. He made a prediction and compared his findings with it. His interpretation, however, is in terms of the conditions rather than in terms of scientific knowledge of why these conditions would cause bread to rot more quickly, as would be expected at level 4.

4.1 Assessment of children's understanding (Part of AT2)

Aspects of work relating to living things in their environment indicating progression from level 2 to level 5:

Level 2: Awareness of the different conditions in local environments and that these affect the living things found there.

Level 3: Identifying ways in which animals and plants familiar to them are suited to their habitats.

Level 4: Using food chains to describe feeding relationships between living things in a habitat.

Level 5: Identifying the factors in different environments which enable different living things to exist there. Explaining why living things may die when changes are made in their habitats.

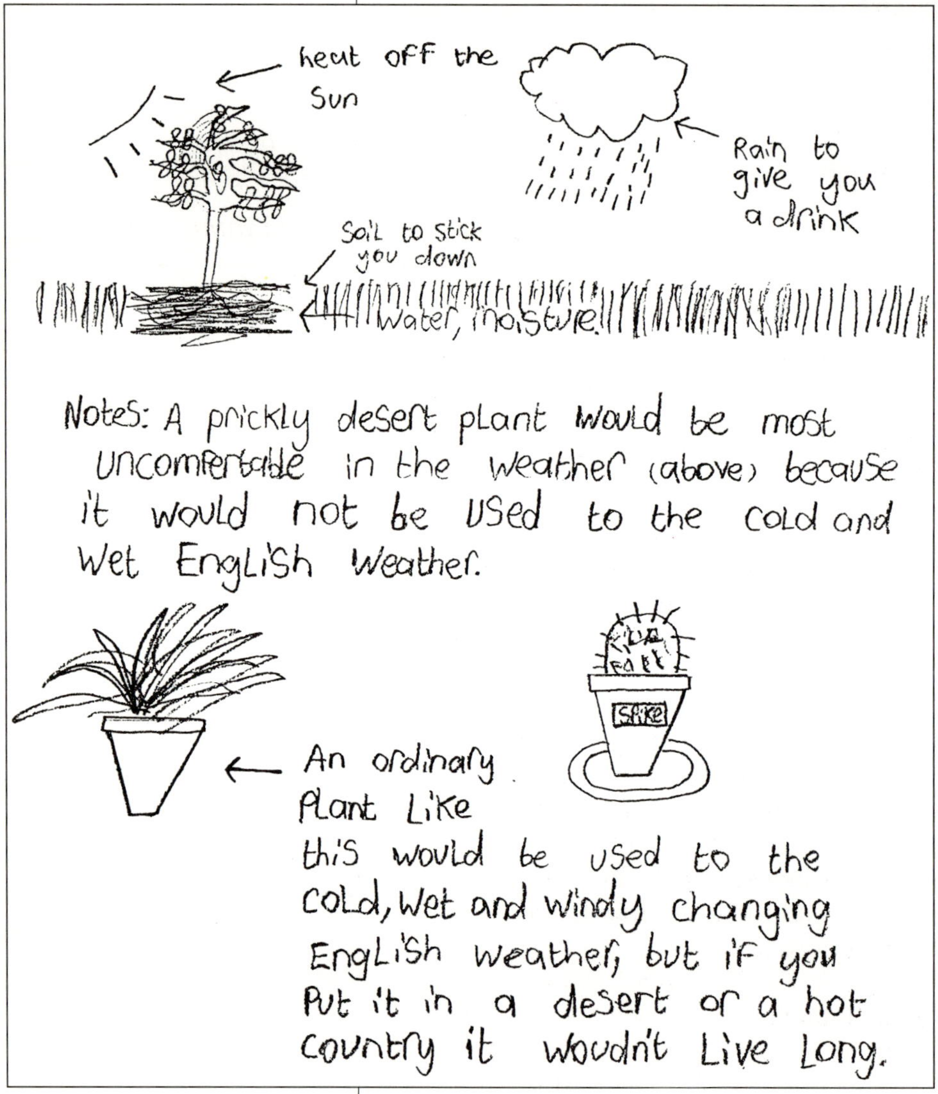

heat off the Sun
Rain to give you a drink
Soil to stick you down
water, moisture.
Notes: A prickly desert plant would be most uncomfertable in the weather (above) because it would not be used to the cold and wet English weather.
Spike
An ordinary plant like this would be used to the cold, wet and windy changing English weather, but if you put it in a desert or a hot country it woudn't live long.

Mark

Mark's annotated drawing demonstrates an understanding of some of the living conditions a plant needs to survive. Mark is clearly aware that different plants need different conditions. He mentions that a house plant could not survive in the desert because the temperature would be too hot.

His work demonstrates an understanding that plants live in different places, and that certain plants are suited to particular conditions.

Although Mark includes the Sun in his drawings, there is no evidence in his work that he appreciates that light is necessary for the survival of green plants. Mark's idea that plants are suited to particular conditions is at level 2. Discussion of the particular features of plants that make them suited to different conditions would help his progress towards level 3.

On pages 40 and 41 we have shown children's drawings of changes in the same habitat in the four seasons. Despite the inaccuracy in indicating that all birds migrate the drawings show clear awareness of changes in the living things related to the environment. Perhaps the children were not fully aware that the survival of the living things in the changing conditions is dependent on their ability to change with it, nonetheless there is certainly evidence of considerable progress towards level 3.

A topic on food and where we get it from led to the work of Rosie, Kameeni, Rebecca and Josh.

Rosie

Kameeni

These drawings indicate a manufacturing process and not a food chain. Both Rosie and Kameeni recognize the importance of plants as a food source, but show how the plants are changed into foodstuffs, rather than their position in a food chain. This work has not yet reached level 4.

Rebecca (overleaf) has attempted to represent a food chain. She is aware that the grass depends on the Sun in order to grow, and the cow depends on the grass for food. She also suggests that some people may eat the cow.

However, there is also a description of how the milk might change into cream and cheese before being eaten. Although Rebecca reveals some confusion in her thinking, her work is moving towards level 4.

Josh (overleaf) has drawn an human's food chain. His description demonstrates an awareness that the Sun has a critical role in the food chain. Josh has shown some understanding of the feeding relationships between living things. His ability to represent this relationship in a food chain indicates that his work is at level 4.

Rebecca

Josh

Jennifer's work shows that she is aware that changes in the environment brought about by humans affect the survival of other living things. She mentions that an oil slick pollutes the sea and describes how birds are affected. She explains that oil on birds' wings prevents the birds from swimming or flying, resulting in their death. Although she should have the opportunity to consider the different ways in which animals and plants are threatened by pollution, her knowledge of how oil pollution affects the survival of sea birds indicates understanding at level 5.

Oil slicks polute the sea. The oil is getting into birds wings and they can't fly or swim. so eventualy they die.

Jennifer

CHAPTER 5

Background science

Habitats and environmental change

Living things are found almost everywhere in the world, be it land, sea or air. Most live in obviously acceptable places, but others live in very extreme situations such as hot, dry deserts, cold polar regions, or springs at very high temperatures. Many living things (such as nits and tapeworms) live on, or in, other living things. The place in which an organism lives is called its habitat and the conditions which exist in its habitat make up the environment.

The environment includes not only the physical conditions (light, temperature, water and so on), but also the other living things that are present. How well a living thing survives in its environment depends on how well it is suited (adapted) to the conditions that exist around it. Generally speaking, the best adapted organisms are the ones which survive, but if they are too well adapted a sudden change in the environment can be devastating. For instance, many New Zealand birds such as kiwis lost the ability to fly because there were no natural predators. With the arrival of humans, the birds were unable to adapt and are now rare. Thus some ability to tolerate changes in the environment can be an advantage to a species.

The habitat in which an organism lives has to provide all its basic requirements: food, water, oxygen and shelter. Plants also require carbon dioxide and light. However, the amounts each organism needs, and the ways in which these requirements are met, vary enormously from organism to organism. Many living things have specific needs: for instance, humans need a supply of vitamins which they obtain from their food; other organisms may need small amounts of particular nutrients, such as calcium, iron, magnesium and nitrogen, to make particular substances for growth.

Living things respond to changes in their environment. This is clearly shown in the way in which many plants close their flowers at night or by birds migrating. Seasonal variation is one of the most obvious examples of how environmental changes influence the growth and behaviour of living things. These changes exert a great deal of control over the life cycle of many organisms and their pattern of growth during the year. For example, this table shows the changes that occur in a deciduous tree during one year.

Season	Environmental conditions	Changes in the tree
Winter	low temperature, short days, low light levels	no leaves, very little activity
Spring	temperatures rise, days lengthen, light levels increase, insect activity increases	new growth starts, buds begin to break, flowers blossom
Summer	temperatures high, long days, good light levels	leaves fully developed, much growth of the tree, flowers die off, fruit seeds start to form
Autumn	temperatures fall, days shorten, light levels decrease, leaves fall	growth slows down, fruits and seeds ripen and fall off

Feeding relationships

Living things in an environment affect each other. They may, for example, compete for space. Birds protecting their territory are establishing the space they need to bring up their family for that year. When food is in short supply animals will compete for it; inevitably, some will die. Large, fast-growing plants will choke less vigorous ones. Although we know that competition occurs between organisms it isn't easy to show it.

A very obvious way in which one organism affects another is by eating it. This is called the predator-prey relationship. We normally think of this as one animal eating another, for example a fox eating a rabbit. However, in biological terms it means an animal feeding off any other living organism – a rabbit eating grass, or a flea feeding off either the fox or the rabbit. If we put these relationships together in a sequence then we have identified a food chain.

A food chain

Energy in the food is passed from one organism to the next throughout the chain. In any given environment food chains are interlinked to make up what is called a food web. A food web summarizes in diagrammatic form all the food chains and feeding relationships for any one environment: a relatively simple food web for a pond is shown opposite.

It is possible to identify a pattern in all food chains and webs. All plants use carbon dioxide, water and light to make their own food by the very complicated process of photosynthesis.

Animals, on the other hand, must get food from elsewhere. Some eat plants (herbivores), some eat meat (carnivores) and others will eat both (omnivores).

All fungi and most bacteria get their food by chemically breaking down dead and decaying matter; they are called decomposers.

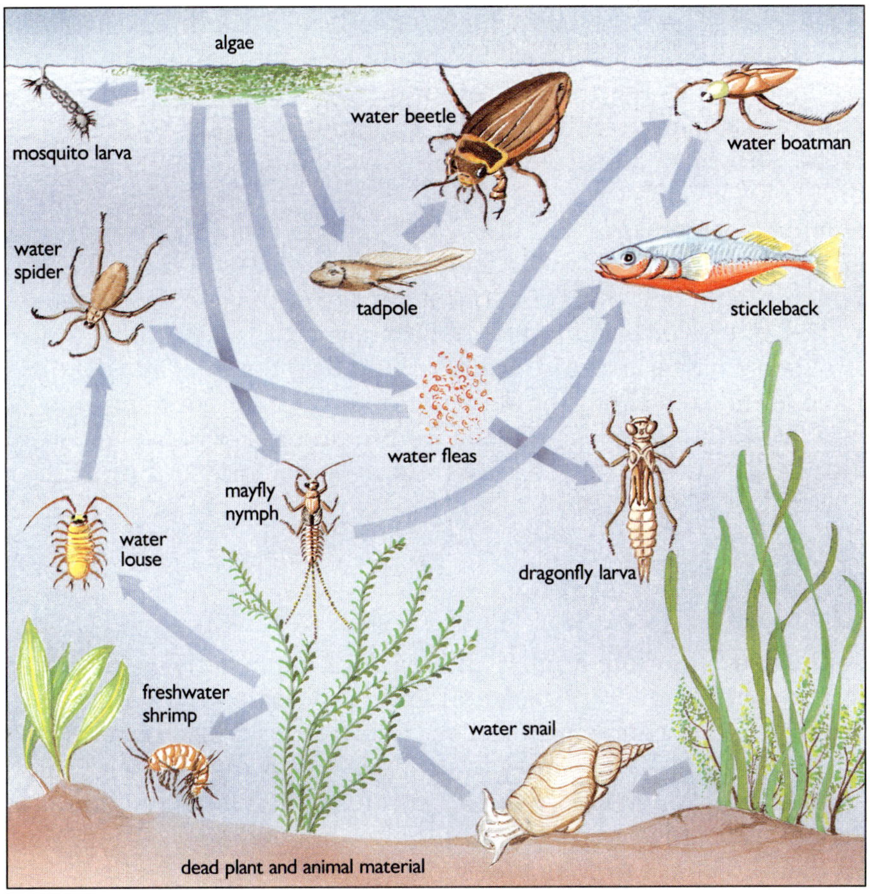

A simple food web in a pond

This means we have another way of grouping living organisms:

Producers:	make their own food	plants and some bacteria
Consumers:		
Herbivores	eat plants	cows, sheep
Omnivores	eat plants and meat	humans
Carnivores	eat meat	cats
Decomposers:	chemically break down dead and decaying matter	fungi and bacteria

The important point to note is that all food chains begin with a producer which is capable of making its food by photosynthesis. The energy for this process comes from sunlight.

Decay

Dead organisms will, in the right conditions, decay so that the material is completely broken down and the substances of which it is made are returned to the environment in an altered form. The process of decay is brought about by bacteria and fungi which release chemicals into rotting material. The reactions which take place break down the solid material into soluble substances. Some of these are then taken in by the bacteria and fungi as their source of food. The remaining substances are dispersed into the environment and are often used again by other organisms. This is a natural process of recycling.

The remains of organisms will decay only in the presence of bacteria and/or fungi. For decay to occur there must be plenty of moisture; it must be warm enough; there must be a supply of oxygen; and chemicals which kill bacteria or fungi must not be present. If the conditions are not suitable for bacteria and/or fungi to function then decay will not take place, or at least it will be slowed down, as it is in a refrigerator. Moisture, warmth and oxygen speed up the process of decay because these things are needed for the growth of most bacteria and fungi.

Waste

Waste is inseparable from almost all areas of human activity and often results in pollution on both the small and large scale. The volume of domestic waste and rubbish produced worldwide varies greatly; in Britain around 20 million tonnes of rubbish are produced each year. Most rubbish is taken away by the local refuse collectors and either incinerated or dumped in large landfill sites before being buried. Both of these methods have problems associated with them.

Incineration of the materials often produces toxic fumes and leaves poisonous ash around. The increasing proportion of plastics in waste adds to this problem.

Some buried materials remain for a very long time without breaking down, while others decay.

Metals corrode and slowly disintegrate. The products of the chemical reactions that take place are released into the soil and make it toxic. Some of these substances may seep into streams and rivers causing damage to natural ecosystems.

Some waste (biodegradable) is decomposed by bacteria and fungi. However, the conditions that exist at a landfill site are not always the most suitable for complete decay to take place. Some poisonous substances and large amounts of the gas methane may be produced. This can build up underground and is a major fire risk. Many landfill sites now have vents fitted into them to release the methane into the air.

Many materials can be re-used (for example, milk bottles) or recycled. Both of these processes help to:

- conserve natural resources;
- save energy in production and transport: recycled goods do not require as much energy to produce and the raw materials do not have to be brought in from abroad;
- reduce the risk of pollution as well as saving costs in its control: if goods are recycled there is less chance that they will be carelessly disposed of with all the attendant problems of disposing of litter;

- reduce the demand for landfill space;
- produce goods more cheaply in the long term.

Much research is being conducted on ways of recycling materials of all kinds. Existing examples include:

- paper: it is estimated that 1 tonne of recycled paper can save 17 trees and over 5 000 kilowatt hours of electrical energy;
- glass: the amount of glass recycled rose from 25,000 tonnes in 1977 to 310,000 tonnes in 1989;
- metal: recycling an aluminium can, for example, uses only about 5 per cent of the energy needed to make one from scratch;
- vegetable matter: composting materials can make a significant saving on the amounts of peat and moss used in gardening;
- old clothes: these can be re-used or recycled for new cloth.

Readily recyclable materials (glass, cans, plastic bottles and paper) account for about 40 per cent by weight of the rubbish thrown out by the average family in a year. In all about 50 per cent is recyclable but at present only about 5 per cent actually is recycled.

People's attitudes towards recycling are perhaps the major factor in its effectiveness. However, the economics of recycling are also significant. Not all forms of recycling are profitable or worthwhile. There is often a fine balance between the availability of waste materials (which have to be collected, sorted and treated) and the price of raw materials. A successful recycling scheme must combine:

- effective collection and sorting of the materials;
- the technology to convert them into a useful product;
- a market demand for the product at an appropriate price.

The effects of human activity on the environment

All living things are influenced by their environment. In turn, all living things affect their environment in some way. However, no other organism has influenced its environment as greatly as the human species, *Homo sapiens*. The ways in which human activities influence the environment are complex and so far-reaching that no part of the Earth has been left unaffected. Pollution has even been detected in the polar ice caps.

As an organism, the human species has the same basic requirements as any other living thing. Humans need a supply of food and water, oxygen, and shelter, and all these requirements are obtained from their surroundings. However, human demands are not restricted to meeting these needs at minimum levels. As humans have become more sophisticated, so have their needs. As a result the local, national and global demands made on the environment have increased with time. This increase has been most rapid in the last 50 to 100 years. For instance, our need for energy has led to the exploitation of many areas of the Earth for oil and has generated much pollution.

The type and intensity of human activity varies from place to place, but there is nowhere on the Earth that has escaped its effects completely. However, it is important at the outset to recognize two points.

Not all human activity is bad for the environment. Work is currently going on in relation to the conservation of particular landscapes, the prevention of soil erosion, the maintenance of species near extinction, the reclamation of derelict land, and so on.

Much of what is said in relation to environmental matters is open to question because it is based on value judgements about what is beneficial, often to a particular group of people; and because the information on which to base opinions may be lacking and/or can be interpreted in different ways. Evidence for the so-called 'greenhouse effect' is based on very limited data and is still questioned by some people.

It is clear that the effects of human activities can be seen in urban, rural and 'natural' areas of the environment. Human activity and its effects can be considered under the following headings.

The use of the environment to provide food

The provision of food is a basic requirement for life. Therefore, the use of land for the production of food has always been a top priority for the human population as a whole. Essentially this is done in two ways:

- by farming, which has changed the landscape itself and created problems through intensive practices and the use of artificial fertilizers and pesticides;
- by fishing, which is now highly mechanized so that many fishing grounds are over-exploited.

The extraction of raw materials

Raw materials of every kind are needed in order to build homes, make roads and manufacture goods. Metals are extracted from ores which are mined, wood comes from forests and plastics are produced from oil. Mining creates large wastes, timber felling can lead to deforestation and erosion of the land, and oil is a precious resource of only limited availability.

Some attempts are being made to limit the damage. For instance, there has been a great deal of research done in recent years to find ways of reclaiming the spoil heaps left by mining operations. Though success has been limited, progress is being made and areas around disused coal mines and slate quarries, for example, have been successfully planted with grasses specifically bred to survive in such harsh soil conditions.

Sources of energy

All activities require energy. The main sources of energy are still the fossil fuels (coal, oil and natural gas). The extraction of each of these affects the local environment, though there are also wider effects to be considered.

The burning of these fuels is a major cause of atmospheric pollution, is responsible for acid rain, and makes a significant contribution to the greenhouse effect. (Sources of energy are also discussed in Chapter 5 of the *Using energy* teachers' guide.)

Housing, transport and industry

Increasing populations with increasing demands for homes, communication systems, tools, machines, vehicles and goods of all kinds have a significant effect on the environment. All these things need raw materials, and energy for their production and use. In addition, people require space for their homes, and so reduce the 'natural' areas of the Earth.

Pollution

This is a very broad term used to describe anything which is likely to have a detrimental effect on the environment. The polluting effect may be made worse when substances are transferred from one place to another, from air to water, or land to water and so on. Acid rain is a good example of this type of pollutant.

In addition, there may be a delay between when a substance enters the environment and the time when its effects are recognized. Such delays may be because the substance enters the environment in only very small amounts but slowly accumulates to the point where its effects can be detected. This is particularly true when chemicals enter the food chain. For example, DDT was used as a pesticide for many years before it was shown to be accumulating in predatory birds and other organisms, numbers of which were declining. DDT is now banned as a pesticide in most countries.

Use of the environment for leisure

An increasing pressure in many countries is the use of the environment for leisure activities. Thus many 'natural' areas are being visited by greater numbers of people who, by their very presence, are causing erosion of the soil and vegetation, as well as reducing the numbers of some animals and plants. The development of facilities such as car parks is further adding to the pressure on the 'natural' environment.

Conservation

Generally, this could be described as a responsible attitude to natural resources and the environment. Such a caring attitude towards the environment and its management and maintenance requires a consideration of the following.

The Earth is a natural system which includes climate, clean air and water, fertile soil, minerals and fuels.

The tropical rainforests have a very delicately balanced ecosystem. If this is disturbed, it is easily destroyed: once the trees have been removed the soil is easily eroded and impoverished so the land becomes almost useless. In addition, the rainforests play a major part in regulating the composition of the Earth's atmosphere and climate. During the process of photosynthesis plants take in carbon dioxide from the air and release oxygen. However, as the expanse of rainforest decreases there is less carbon dioxide removed, which in turn contributes to the increased levels of carbon dioxide in the Earth's atmosphere and the greenhouse effect.

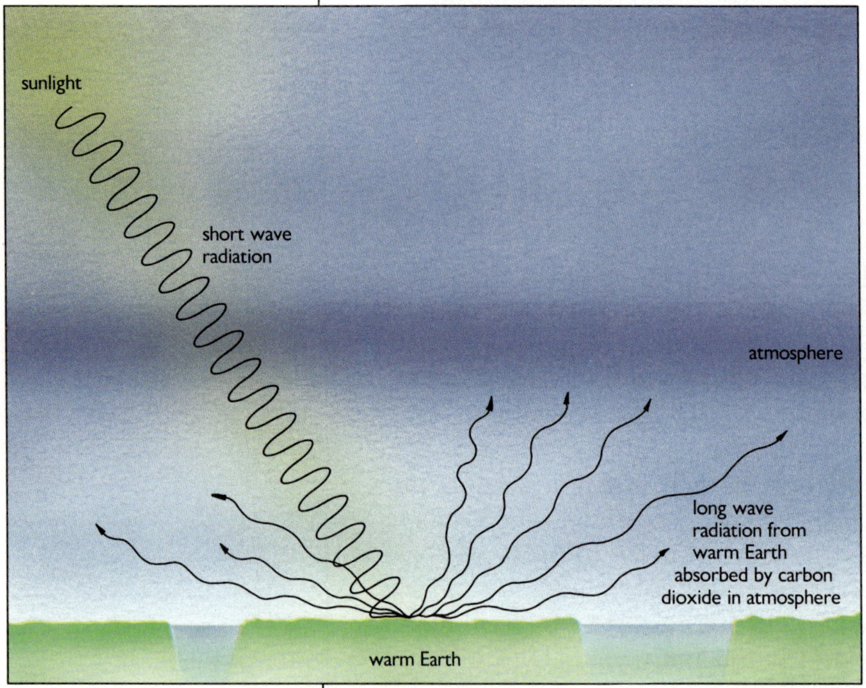

The greenhouse effect

In normal conditions, the greenhouse effect is essential for the survival of life on Earth. The energy from the Sun passes through the atmosphere and causes the Earth to heat up. Some of this energy is re-radiated at a different wave-length and absorbed by carbon dioxide. The atmosphere is not transparent to such radiation so it remains trapped in the Earth's atmosphere and raises the temperature. In this way the temperature of the Earth is maintained. In a balanced system this is an ideal situation. However, the increasing amounts of certain gases (carbon dioxide, methane, CFCs, nitrous oxide and water vapour) that are being released into the atmosphere cause more energy to be retained within the atmosphere. This in turn may lead to an increase in the Earth's temperature (known as global warming). A rise of 1.3 °C is expected by the year 2030. This would cause a rise in sea-levels of nearly 1 metre and the flooding of many low-lying areas around the world. In addition, the climate of many areas would change, with increases in violent storms, typhoons and hurricanes and changes in rainfall patterns.

Other species living on the Earth are used to provide food and medicines as well as aesthetic pleasure; more importantly it is necessary to retain the vast pool of genetic material which these organisms contain and which can be drawn on to improve the quality of food crops and animals.

The interactions between living things, including human beings, and the environment need to be taken into consideration in any future developments.

The human population has a cultural heritage, including buildings, books, artefacts and art.

Global issues

Many human activities are restricted to particular areas, but there is more and more evidence that activities in one part of the world influence other parts as well. Two examples of this are considered here.

Acid rain: the burning of fossil fuels by power stations, certain industrial processes, and car engines releases a complex mixture of gases into the air. In particular, these gases include sulphur dioxide and oxides of nitrogen. In the right conditions in the air these gases combine with water to produce acids such as sulphuric acid and nitric acid. These acids become part of the moisture which eventually falls as rain – acid rain. It is now fully recognized that acid rain does not just fall in the areas that produce the gases, but is carried for hundreds of miles from one country to another. For example, much of the damage to forests in Sweden has been linked to pollution produced in Britain and Germany.

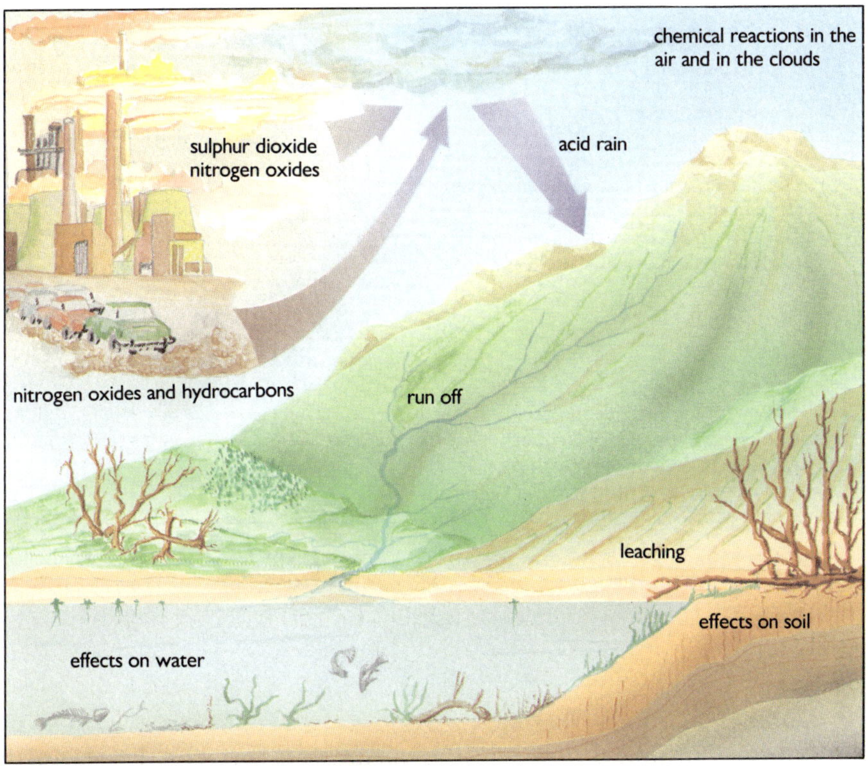

Production of acid rain and its effects

The depletion of the ozone layer: the gas called ozone, which consists of 3 oxygen atoms joined together, is spread thinly in the atmosphere between 10 and 50 kilometres above the Earth's surface. It is essential to all forms of life because it filters out the ultraviolet radiation which comes from the Sun and is harmful to many plants and animals, including humans. For example, the increased incidents of skin cancer have been linked to the higher levels of ultraviolet radiation resulting from the depletion of the ozone layer. Chlorofluorocarbons (CFCs) are a group of chemicals which are used in refrigerators, aerosols, cleaning fluids and expanded plastic such as polystyrene. When they were first invented CFCs seemed to be the answer to many problems, particularly because they are not poisonous and do not burn. They are also very stable and take around 75 years to break down at the Earth's surface. However, in the appropriate conditions they will break down more easily. This seems to happen in the ozone layer, especially in cold conditions. Chlorine is released from the CFCs. When temperatures increase in the spring the chlorine reacts with the ozone to form chlorine monoxide and oxygen. Thus the amount of ozone is decreased. However, the chlorine monoxide is unstable so it splits to give oxygen and chlorine which can then react again with more ozone, and so the cycle is repeated. The more CFCs there are in the atmosphere then the faster the ozone layer will be depleted.

How ozone layer depletion happens

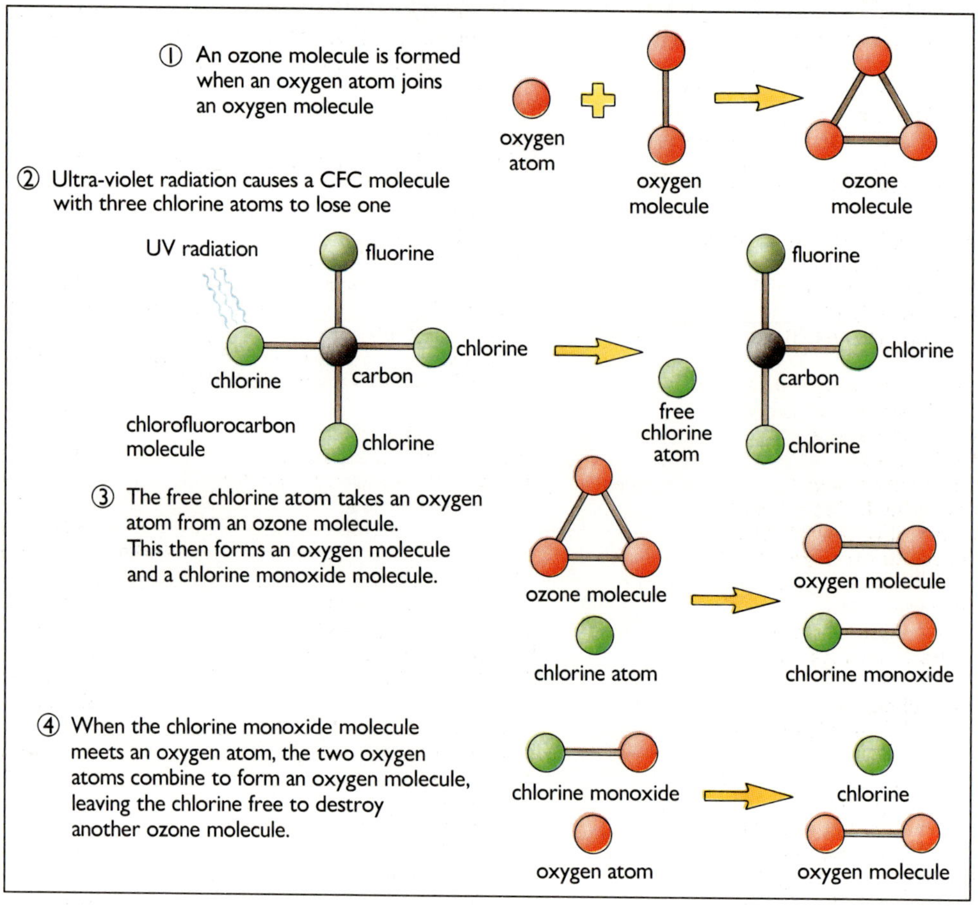
① An ozone molecule is formed when an oxygen atom joins an oxygen molecule
oxygen atom
oxygen molecule
ozone molecule
② Ultra-violet radiation causes a CFC molecule with three chlorine atoms to lose one
UV radiation
fluorine
chlorine
chlorine
carbon
chlorofluorocarbon molecule
chlorine
free chlorine atom
fluorine
chlorine
carbon
chlorine
③ The free chlorine atom takes an oxygen atom from an ozone molecule. This then forms an oxygen molecule and a chlorine monoxide molecule.
ozone molecule
chlorine atom
oxygen molecule
chlorine monoxide
④ When the chlorine monoxide molecule meets an oxygen atom, the two oxygen atoms combine to form an oxygen molecule, leaving the chlorine free to destroy another ozone molecule.
chlorine monoxide
oxygen atom
chlorine
oxygen molecule

Index

Trial schools

The SPACE Project and the Trust are grateful to the governors, staff, and pupils of all the trial schools. It will be obvious to readers of these guides how much we are indebted to them for their help, and especially for the children's drawn and written records of their hard work and their growing understanding of science.

All Saints Primary School, Barnet, Hertfordshire
Ansdell County Primary School, Lytham St Anne's, Lancashire
Bishop Endowed Church of England Junior School, Blackpool
Brindle Gregson Lane Primary School, Lancashire
Brookside Junior and Infants School, Knowsley
Chalgrove JMI School, Finchley, London N3
Christ the King Roman Catholic Primary School, Blackpool
English Martyrs Roman Catholic Primary School, Knowsley
Fairlie County Primary School, Skelmersdale, Lancashire
Fairway JMI School, Mill Hill, London NW7
Foulds Primary School, Barnet, Hertfordshire
Frenchwood County Primary School, Preston
Grange Park Primary School, London N21
Hallesville Primary School, Newham, London E6
Heathmore Primary School, Roehampton, London SW15
Honeywell Junior School, London SW11
Huyton Church of England Junior School, Knowsley
Longton Junior School, Preston
Mawdesley Church of England Primary School, Lancashire
Moor Park Infants School, Blackpool
Mosscroft County Primary School, Knowsley
Nightingale Primary School, London E18
Oakhill Primary School, Woodford Green, Essex
Park Brow County Primary School, Knowsley
Park View Junior School, Knowsley
Purford Green Junior School, Harlow, Essex
Ronald Ross Primary School, London SW19
Rosh Pinah School, Edgeware, Middlesex
Sacred Heart Junior School, Battersea, London SW11
St Aloysius Roman Catholic Infants School, Knowlsey
St Andrew's Roman Catholic Primary School, Knowsley
St Bernadette's Roman Catholic Primary School, Blackpool
St James's Church of England Junior School, Forest Gate, London E7
St John Fisher Roman Catholic Primary School, Knowsley
St John Vianney Roman Catholic Primary School, Blackpool
St Mary and St Benedict Roman Catholic Primary School, Bamber Bridge, Preston
St Peter and St Paul Roman Catholic Primary School, Knowsley
St Theresa's Roman Catholic Primary School, Blackpool
St Theresa's Roman Catholic Primary School, Finchley, London N3
Scarisbrick County Primary School, Lancashire
Selwyn Junior School, London E4
Snaresbrook Primary School, Wanstead, London E18
South Grove Primary School, Walthamstow, London E17
Southmead Infants School, London SW19
Staining Church of England Primary School, Blackpool
Walton-le-Dale County Primary School, Preston
West Vale County Primary School, Kirkby
Woodridge Primary School, North Finchley, London N12